ONWARDS

"Passion for something can easily tip into obsession, which is a dangerous thing, especially when those affected are the very people who so loyally stand and wait."

–Henry Worsley

Published by Doubtful Publishing 2023

Paperback ISBN: 978-1-7384736-0-1
Hardback ISBN: 978-1-7384736-1-8
ePub ISBN: 978-1-7384736-2-5

ONWARDS

DAVID WARREN

Contents

PART 1:

IN THE BEGINNING WAS THE BIRD

"It's fierce, an' it's wild, an' it's not bothered about anybody, not even about me right. And that's why it's great."

Barry Hines, *A Kestrel for a Knave.*

Mike

I first met Mike in 1991. We were both aged nine when a shift in my parents' careers saw my family relocate from Redditch, an urban overspill south of Birmingham, to the unfamiliar surrounds of a remote parish in the rural county of Shropshire. I was nervous and apprehensive when placed into the village primary school, where there were only two classrooms, 46 pupils and just 12 in my year group. My attempts to blend in by wearing Nike tracksuits, oh so common in citified playgrounds, failed dismally. Here, out in the sticks, the kids wore waxed jackets, corduroy trousers, woollen pullovers and even some flat caps. This is not to say they were all posh, with signet rings on their pinkies; they just dressed in simple country attire, clothed for function over fashion and not at all *townie* – the grave insult thrown at me, and used widely by country folk describing townsfolk who know little of rural life and its intricacies. Most of my class were the sons or daughters of nearby farmers. They were growing up in and out of tractors and lambing sheds rather than housing estates and multi-storey car parks. It wasn't long before I discovered that all my classmates followed their parents in undertaking some form of rural pursuit, too. Some followed the South Shropshire Hunt, a lot knew how to fish, and a few went pheasant-beating on the local shoot throughout the winter. All this was utterly foreign to life as I knew it.

✎© April Coppini

My confidence grew one morning after being ushered into the school courtyard alongside the rest of my class. At one end of the quadrangle was a Ford Escort van with its rear doors open. The side of the van was sign-written, advertising the local butcher's shop, Strettondale Meats. Some 20 metres to the rear of the van was a garden fork, stabbed into the ground. Standing next to the fork was Mike, another new boy who had also just joined our class. My first impression was that of a chubby lad, wearing a colourful woollen pullover under a heavily scratched wax jacket. The only thing missing from his countryside apparel was the flat cap. Mike, however, chose a different aesthetic. His was a quiff haircut held firm by his father's Old Spice styling wax – it was a strong look for any nine-year-old. Our teacher, Miss Price, gently pushed the class into a circular shape as we gawped at Mike and tried to peer into the back of the van. Waiting at the rear of the van was Mike's father, Roy. He stood there with a part gurn, part smile, raising his eyebrows and nodding simultaneously at each and every pupil as we eagerly assembled. Roy's arm never left its resting position. He was leant on a wooden box that was lodged just inside the van, held steadfast by the spare wheel and baler twine.

"Right everyone, keep quiet and stay still," cautioned Miss Price.

Mike took his stand by the garden fork and nodded towards his dad, causing everyone to wonder what was going to happen in response to this unspoken cue. Roy moved his arm from the lid of the wooden box and fumbled at the latch. Cautiously, he creaked the door open. The door was only the slightest bit ajar when a piercing whistle from Mike's pursed lips drew our attention. At the same time he raised his left hand and held it high in the air. On his fist, Mike was wearing what I would later learn was his favourite-ever Christmas present: a short-cuff, single-layer Ben Long *Nimrod* leather falconry glove. There, pinched between his thumb and index finger was a dead field mouse, its tail alluringly animated as Mike wiggled his finger back and forth.

Fast as a bullet, a brindle-blurr shot out from the box and streaked across the courtyard towards Mike. Only once this fawn-coloured meteor bound to his glove could we make out the shape of a bird. It was my first-ever encounter with a falcon. Mike calmly introduced the class to his kestrel, Tess. She was indifferent to our presence and confidently began to feed on the pinched field mouse with gruesome vigour. Using her sharp beak, Tess first crunched on the mouse's skull, then bit down hard and pulled the whole torso out from Mike's grasp. With a few gulps the head was swallowed, leaving half the mouse protruding from her beak. Continuing her quaffing motion, the back legs of the mouse then folded neatly and slipped down her throat, and – after some further adjustment and two more gulps – the tail followed suit. Tess then fluffed all her feathers and vigorously shook herself down with buoyant contentment, behaviour which I'd later discover is known as a rouse. I watched on with compulsive fascination as those around me were made queasy by the gorging.

Mike placed Tess on the handle of the garden fork, walked about ten paces away from her, turned, pursed his lips and called her once more to his outstretched fist. He did this a further five or six times before parading her on his fist along the line of awestruck classmates, then returned her to the box in the van. All this time, Roy had stood smiling, bursting with pride.

That was my very first introduction to falconry. If you've ever watched Ken Loach's iconic film *Kes*, then I guess you could say Mike was the Billy Casper of my youth, albeit slightly chubbier and without a Yorkshire accent. Until that point in my life, I had no comprehension of what a kestrel was, let alone any understanding that you could own a bird of prey, train it, and fly it to your fist. From that taster, I was filled with curiosity and hungry to learn everything I could about falconry. I made a deliberate move to sit next to Mike in class so that we'd become best friends, and so that I could glean an insight into his peculiar hobby. Maybe (hopefully) he'd let me fly Tess.

The lesson that cemented our friendship was model-making. We were instructed by Miss Price to work in pairs and build a model car. I was busily constructing, but Mike was disengaged and was desperately trying to think of a way to get out of his evening piano lesson. He eventually concluded that if he hurt his hand, he would have the perfect excuse not to endure an hour of playing scales. Time passed and the end of the lesson drew near. I can't really remember exactly what was said at the time, or what pact was made; all I remember was Mike pushing a whole stick of glue through a hot glue gun onto a sheet of newspaper. The adhesive lay there in hot liquid form and Mike held his fingers over the molten gloop, yet couldn't bring himself to do it. Literally pouncing on the opportunity to help a would-be new best friend, I pushed his hand downwards and held it firmly in the blistering mess. Mike never took another piano lesson, and our friendship was forged. I was excited to have a new best friend.

Our connection grew, and a year later, at age 10, Mike begged his father to let us work in his butcher's shop. With little objection, and the casual disregard for labour laws that was common to farms and rural businesses at the time, we became the Saturday lads at Strettondale Meats. From the start there was no let-up on account of our tender age. We were expected to arrive at the butcher shop at 7am and work through till 6pm, mostly scrubbing floors, washing up and running trays of meat between the shop and the butchery. "You look like a bloody rag-man's cart, time to shape up!" Roy said to me on my first day as he handed over fresh butcher's whites and a clean apron. I put on the uniform and joined Mike in the bakehouse. Roy made us roll up our sleeves above the elbow and ensure we always had clean hands and shoes. From this induction, and after a year or so of learning the ropes, we actually became quite useful, saving many a sausage roll or pork pie from burning in the oven between boxing-up raw-meat orders for the local restaurants.

"Right you buggers, if you're going to be watching these ovens all afternoon, you may as well make the things that go in them," Roy said one morning, having decided it was now time for us to progress. He reached up and pulled his handwritten recipe book off the shelf. It contained his personal recipes, adjusted over the years to create any type of pie or pasty. Our path of righteousness that began saving Roy's sacred pies from burning now extended to making them: game pies, ham and mushroom pies, pork pies, steak and kidney pies, chicken and leek pies, the list went on and on. We went through the ingredients and received instruction on using the mixers, rollers and stamps. After two years of pie-making apprenticeship, at the age of 12, Mike and I were damn near running the bakehouse.

Each Saturday we'd set up a production line. Mike would mix and roll pastry, and I'd then cut, press and line the pie cases. Next, Mike would overtake me to fill the pies, and I'd then overtake him to stamp the lids. Meat cleavers and 8-inch boning knives became the tools of our trade, as we'd get called into the next room to be taught how to joint pig carcasses, skin hams, or make mince and sausage meat. Mike's dad would watch over us and chastise us about our blade technique and the sharpness of our knives. Very often, the knives would be grabbed from our hands and flashed in front of our eyes in a metallic blur as Roy passed them at speed over the sharpening steel. 'Oh arrr. That's it. Better!' Roy said as he tested the sharpness of the knife before handing it back.

Shropshire, an English county located on the Welsh border, has its own quirky dialect – a very rural metre where noises replace words and even entire conversations. *Arrr* in the above context means *yes*, approvingly. Perhaps my favourite use of this phrase occurred not long after we'd started working at the butcher's shop. Mike was especially proud to wear the family uniform, but on this occasion, the apron would be his downfall. I arrived at work and was yet to say hello to him. Mike was nowhere to be seen in the bakehouse, but a loud crash coming from within the walk-in chiller got my attention, so I looked across at the open fridge door. Inside the fridge, Mike had tripped when his butcher's whites snagged on the shelving unit inside. His attempt to untangle the apron was made nearly impossible due to the fact he was carrying a rather heavy pig. Mike had unhooked the beast from the sky rail and had it balanced on his shoulder when he attempted to walk out of the chiller and became snared. The pig's body length exceeded the width of the fridge door, so Mike was unable to turn around and address the problem. Each time he went back and forth in a bid to untangle the snagged apron, the pig's head would appear, then disappear, before reappearing from behind the door. The disgruntled, cuckooing pig spoke in escalating swearwords.

"Alright bo?" I asked, after he eventually untangled himself. Mike walked straight past me into the butchery, and from the far side of the charioted pig, he shouted, "Arrr."

We were not paid to giggle or fool around. Roy kept us firmly in check and we were unable to leave until we had washed down the bakehouse at the end of the day. The bakehouse had to be immaculate, and the pastries had to be perfect, as did the cups of tea we were obliged to make throughout the day. "Mind you brew it right, none of that bloody ditch-water you served last time," Roy would say in an attempt to safeguard the standard of his next cup.

Roy would never accept the pathetic excuses we'd offer up for not making a decent cup of tea and we quickly learned it was sacrilege to do otherwise. On one occasion we forgot ourselves (let's blame our youth, after all we were only 12 years old) and decided to play a prank on Roy. Mike submerged an egg in the cup of tea he had made for his dad. We called Roy through to the bakehouse for his brew and he stood with us making small talk about quiches as he supped. Unbeknown to us at the time, Roy wasn't in the best of moods, and with every sip of tea let out more choice expletives, berating customers and soggy flans. With each slurp we became increasingly nervous as we realised the gravity of our stupidity, yet neither of us broke our complicit silence to warn him. Roy continued to drink, but the egg remained – remarkably – unnoticed. The circumference of the egg must have perfectly fitted the china cup, and somehow held steadfast under the water. Roy put the cup to his lips and tipped it up a little further. The egg came unstuck, bopping him on the nose as hot tea poured on his face and subsequently down his butchers' whites. "What the bloody hell!" Roy exclaimed as he looked up to see two boys, unable to contain themselves, giggling at him. "That's it, you boys have just buggered your contract!"

The cup was smashed on the floor next to the fallen egg, blue expletives silenced our laughter and Roy stormed out of the bakehouse. It was not our finest hour, and serious reparation work was needed. At the end of the day, Roy cashed up the register then came through to inspect the bakehouse. He pointed out everything he found unsatisfactory with our work that we would need to rectify before he'd let us go home. His list was substantial. On this occasion I'd failed to thoroughly clean under the large pastry roller, and flour lay like confetti on the floor. My excuse was that I couldn't reach the mess and naively hoped Roy might then overlook it. Roy grimaced before he drew a massive wedge of folded £20 and £50 banknotes from his pocket, the likes of which I'd never seen before. "You'd bloody manage to reach down there if this was on the floor with your name on it," He was right; of course I would have, so I nodded. Roy smiled in agreement before he continued. "Well that'll never happen, so I suggest you get reaching down there with your bloody broom and try and earn it instead."

It was certainly character building. With a taste for earning money and an entrepreneurial mindset, Mike and I set about the local villages every Sunday and washed cars to add to the £10 we'd each earned for that 11-hour shift at the butcher shop. On reflection, I'm not too sure why we pushed so hard to earn money given that we didn't really want for much or have expensive tastes. We'd amuse ourselves by building camps in the local woods, ride our bikes round the village. We never chased computer games, clothing labels, cassettes or luxuries. That said, whoever said *money doesn't buy happiness* has never bought themselves a new fishing rod. Mike and I often pooled our money and would take the train into Shrewsbury, purely to look around the fishing tackle shop. Here we'd spend hours inspecting the shiny spinners and lures, deciphering which one might tempt a monster from the depths. In reality, we were purchasing decorative ornaments that would end up snagged in the trees that overhung the trout ponds of Church Stretton each time our casting went awry. If we weren't buying lures, we'd spend our hard-earned cash purchasing pints of maggots and day tickets to fish the local lakes of South Shropshire, inconveniencing our parents by begging them to drop us at the lakeside at dawn and collect us just before nightfall. When money was tight or there was no one to take us fishing, we'd dig for worms and head to the nearest stretch of water to where I lived, the river Onny, for a brown trout. While we enjoyed fishing expeditions and grafting at the butchery, the thing I loved the most and always hoped for was to stay at Mike's house for a chance to fly his kestrel.

Mike and Tess ~1992 📷©Dave Warren

Reverend Payne

Home was a large, greystone, former rectory adjoining the graveyard of Wistanstow Church, Shropshire. It was quite a daunting, spooky place for any young boy to grow up, but I soon learned to love it. In order to get to the village primary school, I had to cross the churchyard. The underlying earthy smell that would greet me as I walked through the church gates and crossed the graveyard on my way to school became all too familiar. The musk was most obvious directly after a rain shower on a warm spring day. The rising sun caused the ancient stone walls that surrounded the church boundary to heat up, and a dank odour cadged a lift on the evaporating mist that clung over the graveyard. It was always a quiet place at that time in the morning when I walked alone to school. I would regularly stumble upon recent burial plots covered by an array of fresh flowers. Sometimes you'd smell the flowers first, knowing the piece of corrugated tin you'd lifted earlier in the week to peek into a six-foot grave hole would no longer be there. Instead, the grave would now be filled with corpse, coffin and clay.

Occasionally, I'd meet the gravediggers as they cut downwards with their spades. But more regularly, if I stood in the right place in the churchyard each week, I'd hear the expectant jangling of keys followed by a familiar voice. "I'm heading up if you want to join me?" It was the parish vicar, Reverend Payne, crossing the graveyard. He was pointing at the top of the church tower with one hand and clutching a giant set of keys in the other, en route to wind the clock mechanism.

I followed Reverend Payne up the narrow sandstone stairwell to the top of the bell tower. It was my favourite vantage point from which to view the village. I got a teasing image each time I passed the slotted windows as I climbed higher up the tower. I would then climb a rickety ladder that led to the battlements at the very top to survey the hamlet. There, my vivid imagination would run wild, and my mind conjured German Messerschmitts flying overhead, firing down onto the church. With each turn of the key, Reverend Payne and the clock mechanism provided the backing track to accompany my daydream. The ratchet struck each tooth of the gear as the huge weights of the clock were lifted. This emitted a fast rhythmical beat –

clack, clack, clack – as the striking irons echoed the sounds of imaginary guns rattling off rounds at villagers fleeing the safety of the church.

Once the clock was wound and it was time to leave, I'd sprint from the church back to the safety of home. I'd time my leaps to perfection, hurdling over the graves before the Messerchmitts had a chance to return. I'd do my best to dodge the gravestones and jump high to clear the mounded soil, although I was guilty, on more than one occasion, of unintentionally leaving size-6 footprints in the fresh topsoil covering a recent burial. Mouse holes along the cemetery path were the bullet holes from aircraft, while the fallen Yew berries laid across the pathway were the bloodied, splattered remains of fallen soldiers.

Wistanstow Church 📷©Colin Canfield

I think many young boys of my generation grew up with stories from WWII, and as such developed an imaginative warring mind-set. For me, the messages were mixed. We learned about World War II in primary and secondary school, role-playing evacuations, and being instilled with pride as we covered resilience in the Blitz, the miracle of Dunkirk, and the inspirational bravery of Spitfire pilots. I probably also watched far too much *Dad's Army*, buoyed by its fun portrayal of the war, rather than understanding the horrific atrocities that actually occurred. It was my grandparents who imparted the most profound lessons. I had an excited interest in and a romanticised notion of being in wartime battle. Yet the only personal anecdote from the battlefields of World War II was from my grandfather, Capt. Webb, Royal Army Service Corps. I think I must have been about 8 years old when I asked, "Tell me about the war, Granddad." My grandfather tightened his eyes and, with a slow shake of the head, replied: "The war was a terrible, terrible thing."

He died when I was 12, and in all my efforts spent as an adult trying to remember him and the conversations we had, these were the only words I *distinctly* remember him saying to me. If that was the one thing he wanted to impress on my young enquiring mind, he had achieved it.

Captain C. Webb. Norway ~1945 📷©Dave Warren

I was fortunate to have more opportunities to converse with my grandmother, who was born in 1912, and who outlived my grandfather by more than 20 years. She could clearly recall the day that the Great War ended in 1918, as it also happened to be her sixth birthday. As she stood with her mother and looked out at the fireworks, she was scared of the bangs, but her mother reassured her that it was a day of joy. Given her name was

Joyce, Joy for short, she made the logical conclusion that the fireworks were for her birthday! However, from that year onwards, the 11th of November became Remembrance Day, and she downplayed her birthday out of respect. On turning 100 years old in 2012, she had her rightful party, and was as pleased as Punch to receive a card from the Queen. Her resilience and fierce independence, like so many of that generation, stemmed from a cruel period of uncertainty, austerity and survival. I lost count of just how many times she told us grandchildren to *make do and mend*, angered at times by our imprudence. During my grandfather's 1945 posting to Norway, he received an invitation from a Norwegian couple following a plea to welcome British forces into their homes. He discovered there was precious little to share, and more troubling, the wife of the couple was heavily pregnant, and, with good reason, worried about how to clothe and provide for the baby. "The family hadn't a single thing to put on the baby's back – no clothes, no anything," Grandma told me. She had received a letter from my granddad explaining the situation. Feeling compelled to help, she rallied round all her friends who had babies, gathered all the baby clothes she could and made a parcel that she sent through the army for safe passage. In clearing the house after her death in 2014, we found a box containing wartime effects: my grandfather's medals, trench whistles, and a letter from Norway dated 12th November 1945, which read:

… I don't know in which way I shall thank you for the wonderful package Margit and I got from you. It was too much and because of my bad English I can't explain what I feel, but you have to understand that many deep feelings are included in the little word, Thanks!

… In our newspapers we could had an appeal that Norwegians should invite Allied officers and soldiers to their homes, for in that way try to make it a little easier for them…. Now he comes without a written invitation, and we are glad for that and have to drink a cup of coffee and if we have cake he get some, if not he has his dear pipe. We speak of everything in the world and if only a little percent of our proposals would have been practised the world would have been wonderful to live in.

****

It was mid-afternoon, late in November 1991. I was still adjusting to my new surroundings. The old farm track leading to our house was a far cry from the new-build housing estate in Redditch. I remember feeling extremely disgruntled that my radio-controlled car, which had worked so beautifully on the rolled tarmac paths of suburbia, was now struggling with the unmade stone track that surrounded the graveyard. Aggressively, I kicked loose stones off the mud path leading up to the Old Rectory and got myself into a bit of a state. At that point, Reverend Payne's Volvo 340 bundled into view and came to a stop. Watching my haplessness from behind the wheel, I imagine Reverend Payne must have taken pity on me. As such, he offered an alternative activity and invited me to jump in and go duck flighting with him. Clueless as to what this would entail, I begged my parents to let me go with the Reverend. My parents agreed – on the condition that I would be back before nightfall, probably because they, too, hadn't the slightest idea what duck flighting involved. With us all assuming that the vicar was taking me to feed some local ducks, I jumped into the passenger seat of his Volvo and headed out of the village. It was about half an hour before sunset and we arrived on the outskirts of Cheney Longville, a small village close by. I remained clueless and stood to one side as Reverend Payne unpacked the car. He didn't give much away as he handed me some plastic ducks, a bundle of camouflage netting, a thermos flask, and a small leather bag.

"Don't drop that bag," he instructed jokingly, presumably to liven me up. I was unsure why it amused him to say that; maybe he felt a need to lighten the mood. His quip served little purpose other than to confuse me further. I had no idea what was in the leather bag – bread and corn presumably – So why was it so precious and [why was it] causing such amusement to him? Next, he reached into the rear seats of his Volvo and drew out a set of dark, metallic shotgun barrels. The slow extraction of the gun alarmed me. I felt conflicted. In my head I was listening to my mother's warning tones: "*Guns are bad, never go near or touch them.*" Yet I remained transfixed with curiosity. It was the first time I'd seen a shotgun – any gun – and memorably breathed in the unforgettable (now much loved) bouquet of dank wax jacket and gun oil. My reverence for the Reverend, standing before me with his shotgun, was quite something, but – although a little uneasy – I wasn't frightened.

"Are we actually going to shoot ducks?" I asked in amazed uncertainty. "Is a vicar even allowed to do this?" was my follow-up question, to which Reverend Payne laughed. "Well, that depends. Are you a good shot?" His response came as he rushed me through the gate and marched at pace across the field. He was focused on the bruising skyline. "No," I said, trying to keep up. Unsurprisingly, this small boy had never shot a duck. Was I supposed to have done so? Feeling a little uneasy, I did my best to put on a brave face and act nonchalant as we stumbled on.

"Well I'll do all the shooting, you can be in charge of the 'quacker'. It's your job to call the ducks in. You'll hear them before you see them. I'll explain everything in a bit, we're nearly there now. Come on – keep low."

I followed the whispering, hunched-over shape of Reverend Payne as he crept down a hawthorn hedgerow. Being half his height, I simply remained upright and carried the bags. We arrived at a small lily-covered pond that lay adjacent to the slow-running River Onny. We squelched forward towards two old wooden transport pallets standing upright about 6 feet apart. "Quick, put all the kit behind the pallets and help me stretch the net out." These were Reverend Payne's softly spoken orders as he rested his gun on the leather bag and threw the hessian sack containing the plastic ducks down behind a pallet. He set about frantically untangling the camouflage netting as I dutifully held my two corners, and between us we stretched it out, assembling our makeshift hide. "Right, throw these ducks into the pond. Throw them as far as you can, they'll float back to the side with the wind so we can pick them up later. Hurry! – we need to get ourselves hidden."

As I flung half a dozen plastic ducks into the pool, Reverend Payne grabbed the leather bag. Intrigued as to what was inside, I watched him open it and remove what looked like a mini rubber accordion with a plastic horn attached. He passed it to me then reached further into the bag, grabbed a couple of shotgun cartridges and began stuffing them into the barrels of his gun. I assumed my position behind the left-hand pallet, looking down at this accordion-like device. "You need to make two slow calls, followed by five much shorter, quicker calls," Reverend Payne said whilst he dropped two cartridges into his gun. The clinking of the cartridges against the barrels was followed by a solid clunk as he closed the stock. He was now poised, looking skyward to the horizon, hiding behind the pallet and gripping his shotgun.

I gently stretched the device, and squeezed it together twice as instructed, *Quaaack, Quaaack.* Then I stretched the device out once more, but this time squeezed it together in five sharp motions: *qua-qua-qua-qua-quack.* "Perfect, you're a natural. Do that every time I put my thumb up," Reverend Payne said with a surprise that tore his focus from the skyline, impressed with my decoying skills. I repeated the quacks, and remained perfectly still. Breaking the silence, overhead somewhere, I heard the fast rhythmical whistling of wingbeats and looked up to see if I could spot the… BANG! BANG!

Reverend Payne had shot both barrels, which caused me to jump out of my skin. Before I could regain composure, there was a big splash, and I found myself looking to the middle of the pond. I traced the ripples back to their epicentre to see what looked like a floating log. It was of course a dead duck, head drooped under the water and motionless. Reverend Payne quickly dropped two more cartridges in his gun, snapped his barrels shut and returned to his hunched position behind the pallet. The ripples from the crashed duck made all the decoys bob up and down and become animated. It was as if these plastic ducks had somehow been sent into a frenzy by what they had just witnessed. I, however, remained composed and unflustered. In fact, I remember feeling disappointed that I somehow missed seeing everything unfold. But I now knew the sound of the gun and when to anticipate the bangs. Now I could pay attention and see another duck come in, I did my best with the quacker to entice more whistling wings.

I was left in charge of the quacker for the rest of the night. It was thrilling to call wild ducks from the river. It proved to be one of the most influential nights of my life. I loved every minute of learning how to lure ducks, laying perfectly still and silent, listening for wings whistling overhead under the bright moon. It was at this point that my eyes and ears first opened to the sensory zeal of the natural world.

In the countryside, sounds can have a beautifully overwhelming effect. In an urban environment, the traffic, industry and bustle create a backdrop of white noise. In the countryside, the only white noise is the wind, leaving space for the sounds of nature to puncture it. Stags bellowing, snipe winnowing, grouse lekking, carp lip-smacking on slow-moving mill ponds. The suspense and anticipation become addictive, and when you attune to them, they stir your soul.

©April Coppini

We drove home. Next to my feet in the passenger footwell were half a dozen bloodied Mallard ducks. "Careful not to stand on them, they'll need to cool off overnight. Well, what did you think?" Reverend Payne asked.

"It was brilliant, but isn't God going to be upset with us?" I responded. Having been educated in Church of England primary schools, and never having intentionally killed anything other than a wasp, this was quite a big consideration. The ducks were beautiful creatures, and any similarities between them and the roast chicken that graced my Sunday dinner was beyond my youthful moral comprehension.

"I don't believe so, no. God is like a bull elephant: hard to explain, but you'd know if he was upset with you. You can take a duck home to eat, but remember to pray before eating it. "Just say, 'rub-a dub-dub, three cheers for *the grub'*." Needless to say, I didn't make it home before nightfall – we would have missed all of the sport! In the darkness, I stumbled out of Reverend Payne's Volvo and up the garden path. My boots were muddied, hands bloodied, yet I was grinning from ear to ear and proudly holding up the dead duck – to no ovation. I could tell from the look on my father's face that he was waiting for Reverend Payne to depart so he could then reprimand me for blasting ducks past my bedtime. Mercifully, I was given a stay of execution when my elder sister, Rebecca, suddenly appeared. She was returning from an evening of childminding, having looked after a young boy called Max. Max was the son of the village newcomers Henry and Joanna, and my parents were keen to find out more. The village knew little, if anything, about the newcomers.

*****

Henry

Henry and Joanna had just moved to Wistanstow. Joanna stunned the weathered farmhands and stockmen who lived in the village with her rich chestnut, shoulder-length hair, slim figure, glowing eyes and Mediterranean complexion. She was married to Henry, a slim and athletic man, handsome, with boyish good looks and the most piercing, warm blue eyes you could ever wish to be fixed by. The busied and flurried questioning of my sister allowed me to kick off my muddy boots in the porch and skulk upstairs without reproach. Once my sister finished her questioning, she came upstairs to find me and asked, "What are you doing on Saturday?"

"Not a lot!" was my grunted reply.

"Well, you've got to meet Henry, he wanted to know if you'd like the job of looking after his ferrets when he goes on holiday."

"*Really?*" I said excitedly.

"Why not? I'm babysitting for them, but I don't know about ferrets. Henry says he'll come and find you."

The prospect of being appointed to the important position of ferret keeper excited me. I longed to have a dog, but this was simply untenable with both my parents working full-time. I thought a ferret would be a compelling equivalent. It would be another exciting new experience with a creature I knew nothing about. I was keen for more opportunities to pry into the animal kingdom and it looked like becoming a ferret keeper was my next best chance. I was determined to make it a success, so I needed to prepare. *I've heard of a ferret, but what exactly **is** a ferret?* I asked myself. I went into my father's study, walked along his line of books, past photography albums, bird books, copies of national geographic journals, then drew out an old encyclopaedia and opened it up – Mustela putorius furo *translates as fierce and smelly*, it read. *A small mammal, domesticated from the polecat to hunt rabbits.* Thank goodness it had a picture. I didn't know what a polecat looked like either. A polecat sounded like something I should be very scared of, especially living next to a graveyard. A feline type of a hellhound, perhaps? It didn't bear thinking about, but the domestic version – the ferret – sounded excellent, and I was keen to investigate.

Riding my bike in the village a few days later, Henry caught me unawares when he pulled up alongside me in his E-Type Jag in British Racing Green. Henry was keen to strike a deal. He would take me rabbiting providing that I looked after his ferrets whenever he had to go away, which might be at a moment's notice. It was a done deal. "You know where I live, pop round and see me in the morning." Henry thanked me, smiled, then accelerated out of the village, leaving me sitting on my bike engulfed by rich petrol fumes and the echoes of upshifting gears. I admired his shiny E-Type as it disappeared down the lane. It was a stunning car and quite different to mother's small yellow Renault Clio that my sister and I fondly nicknamed 'the banana car'.

It was bitterly cold on what I now know was the perfect morning for ferreting. My feet were already freezing in my wellies as I walked round the corner to Henry's house. The frost-covered cast-iron handle of the gate snapped open, but the rusted wrought-iron Coalbrookdale gate held firm. The gate was intertwined with ivy and held fast. This roadblock was all that separated me from my newfound ambition of becoming a ferreter and, not realising there was a simpler way into the garden, there was nothing for it but to ignorantly push harder. "No need to fight the gate – you'll come off second best," came Henry's voice. "Second place is first loser – remember that." Henry then nipped into his shed and reappeared next to me on the roadside with a bag of nets, a folding trench-shovel, a shotgun, and an old army ammo box containing two ferrets scratching loudly at the air holes drilled into the top of the box. The day was set to be an unassailable first lesson in field craft, net-setting and catching rabbits.

Henry pulled the neatly folded purse nets out of the canvas bag and taught me how to set them. First, the peg went in at a 45-degree angle on the topside of the hole. This creates the strongest possible anchor. The net is then opened in a big round shape to cover the entire rabbit hole. Henry gave me his secret tip: to lightly flick the bottom bit of the net down into the hole, so that the bolting rabbit has its front feet planted on the fold of the net before its head hits the crux of it. The rabbit's momentum then closes the net around itself as it flees the warren – securing the tangled rabbit tightly within. "Guaranteed rabbit pie, every time," Henry said as he finished his lesson.

Doing my best not to make a sound, I crept round the half-a-dozen holes, netting them as per Henry's instructions when he declared, *"It's a can of coke forfeited if a rabbit gets away."* He smiled as he made the wager and took the ferrets out of the ammunition box. This was the first time I'd laid eyes on one. It was a female, which are known as jills. Henry lifted the slinky, sandy coloured, elongated rat-like creature out by the shoulders, leaving her long torso, back legs and furred tail swinging underneath while the pointy, whiskered nose and inky black eyes were held high. He walked to the edge of the warren, lifted the net out of the way and slipped the ferret down the rabbit hole. After a short while, Henry's face lit up. He smiled at me, beckoned me over and made me kneel next to one of the holes. Without a moment to realise what was happening, he pushed my head down into the rabbit hole, my temple scuffed raw with earth, and he excitedly whispered, "Just listen". Then I heard it, the underground thunder, the sound created by his ferret doing its best to bolt a stubborn, reluctant rabbit. That same rumble, even today, sends electricity down my spine. Eventually, the rabbit made a bid for freedom and ran straight into one of Henry's nets. Scooping up the rabbit in the net, he showed me how to untangle it by holding its back legs with the left hand, then, using the right hand, how to arch its head back and instantly dispatch it by breaking its neck in one sharp motion.

The whole incident happened in seconds. The rabbit gave a quick struggle in the net before being scooped up and held firm. Whilst I deliberated and wondered if the rabbit was in pain or not, it had already been dispatched. It happened so fast that I thought Henry had accidently dropped the rabbit; instead he had thrown down the stone-dead torso and was quickly resetting the net.

Just like the duck, the rabbit lay motionless. Their deaths were instant, neither creature was left writhing in pain or agony, and I think that was the key to my accepting these pursuits. I had no chance to form an emotional connection to the quarry. Sure, each was cute and fluffy, but their dispatch was so clinical and quick that it didn't seem cruel. We continued netting and working the network of tunnels along Horderly Bank until we came across a large warren twisting underneath a gorse and juniper thicket, making it impossible to set the nets. Henry instructed me to stand behind him as he unzipped the gun case and loaded his shotgun. "No one likes explaining they shot the vicar, not the terrorist." Henry said with a smile on his face as he stood in front of me. The jill then proceeded to dance her jig, bleating in excitement as she scurried and danced in delight around the thicket, chasing the scent of rabbit and producing bolting targets for Henry to take aim at.

Henry and I spent a lot of time ratching around South Shropshire looking for warrens as he patiently taught me fieldcraft. On one of our excursions, as I waited expectantly at the iron gates for Henry to appear, he shouted over "Just one more thing I need to bring with us today." He took himself into the house and returned with a baby carrier. In it was his son, Max. "If we keep ourselves quiet and Max upright, he should sleep for the duration." So the three of us set off, Max sleeping soundly for the short car journey, only stirring briefly as he was lifted from the rear seat. Trussed-up in a thick jacket with a few wisps of golden-brown hair poking through his woolly hat, Max soon resumed his recumbent slump.

"This looks like a likely spot." Henry pointed to some freshly dug rabbit holes running through the roots of a huge oak tree. He took some paracord from his pocket, tied the baby-carrier to the tree, and we carried on our business. As we scurried around setting nets and scooping up bolting rabbits in perfect silence, Max was sleeping obliviously, trussed up in the tree.

A few weeks passed before Henry had to go away at short notice. It was time to honour my side of the bargain and look after his ferrets. Joanna was in London for the week, so I was given a key to their home and instructed where to find the ferret food and wood shavings. I opened the front door to their home and went down the main corridor, heading straight for the kitchen. I only took half a dozen steps when I stopped in my tracks. On the walls, shelves and everywhere I looked were the most amazing photographs of Henry, soldiering in the Army. There were pictures of him sat on Land Rovers in the desert, jumping from aircraft carriers, running out of helicopters, hunkered in the jungle in full camouflage. I was in complete wonderment; you can imagine the excitement I felt sneaking round the downstairs, looking at photographs in complete awe.

Annoyingly for me, his life in the Special Air Service inevitably took Henry away from the village and onto more high-octane adventures. I lost connection with my boyhood hero, but I never lost his influence. He had given me my first ferret. Not only was she my first ever pet, but to this day she has been the best working ferret I've ever owned or seen. I cried for days when she died of parvovirus and buried her beneath a tree in view of the rectory. I'll go back there one day.

Me, ferreting. ~ 1994 📷©Dave Warren

*****

The Unsolicited Envoy

It was 1996. Mike and I had two years left in comprehensive school when, despite all attempts to be discreet, our teacher crashed through the door and unwittingly spread disorder in our home economics class. Maybe it was the raw, tear-shot eyes and pale shaking hands, or maybe it was the sheer burden she carried that made this unsolicited envoy so clumsy. She continued determinedly, grabbed 14-year-old Mike by the bicep, turned and frog-marched him out of the classroom.

"Well, it's one less Christmas present to buy," was Mike's response upon returning to our table some 5 minutes later. He was dour and deliberate, not making eye contact. I suspect he didn't want us to know that he was hurting. Removing the HB pencil from behind his ear he tapped it on the desktop, just as a drummer would mark the punch line of a terrible joke and, after hitting an empty pineapple tin like a cymbal, threw the pencil to the floor and walked out of the lesson.

About a week or so later I arrived at the small, quaint church in Leebotwood for Mike's mother's funeral. The church was already full, so I joined some friends standing in the churchyard next to an external speaker that relayed the vicar's voice. The sun was warming and the breeze was calm. More people joined to listen to the service, hymns were sung, and then the Church began to empty, nearest and dearest first. Those standing outside made off the path and stood sympathetically to one side to allow free passage to the funeral cars. It was quite a tunnel of people and must have been quite daunting for Roy, Mike, his brothers and sisters to walk along. Where do you look? Selfishly I remained head bowed to keep any emotional outbursts in check. I knew I'd be fine unless I looked up to see my best friend hurting. Taking a few deep breaths and not being too sure of what to do with myself, I started to walk out of the church yard. Most people went left to the car park, but I turned right and quietly walked to the village to catch a bus home. A loud and frantic knocking on a car window suddenly got my attention. I looked back down the lane to see the funeral cortege driving away slowly. As I squinted through the blacked-out glass of the lead funeral car I could see Mike desperately trying to get my attention. Mike frantically pointed forward with his right hand whilst miming drinking with his left. Mike pointed again towards the direction of Leebotwood village and The Pound Inn, his beaming face nodding excitedly as the car passed the end of the road and I lost sight of him. I bet if there was an emergency brake lever Mike would have wrenched it and invited me in for a lift. After such antics, neither of us needed a brave face or forced composure. Within three minutes I had walked into the local pub and shared another underage pint of Woods' 'Shropshire Lad' with my best friend.

Remarkably, or maybe not for the time, Mike only had two days leave from school over the entire episode of his mother's terminal bowel cancer. These were the day after her passing, and the day of the funeral. Mike was given no time off or means to grieve for his mother. Instead, he was expected to retain a stiff upper lip. At just 14 years old, I was not emotionally mature enough or aware of what effect watching his mum die of cancer would have on my friend. There was no guide book or provision from school to help Mike, and to a lesser degree, me. What should a young adolescent boy say or do in this situation? With no guidance forthcoming, we just made it up. In the months that followed we did our best to stand tall, and at the most inappropriate times, fall into fits of uncontrolled laughter, as is only possible with that one true friend.

Mike had no option but to grow up fast. I still had the securities of a family home, yet Mike was forced to become bolder, braver and more independent. Like all young bucks, over the next couple of years, we began to take ownership of our interest and kept ourselves amused over the long summer holidays. As we punched through our teenage years, we were now looking at life beyond the confines of the school gates and parental control. Mike moved from his childhood home to a remote farmhouse with Roy, his brothers and sister. The house was located one mile down an unmade track, surrounded by fields and a good distance from the nearest village, Smethcott. In the summer, when we were not required at the butcher's shop, we'd find work farming, lambing and fruit picking. At 16 years old, we also had a new objective: earning enough money to skulk to the pub and find girls. The closest pub to serve us, The Bottle and Glass at Picklescott, was some three miles and a hour-long hearty walk away from Mike's house. The barman of a weekend was a retired policeman called Sid, who, for reasons unknown, wore a toupee. Perhaps it was our bold approach or maybe his hair-brained indifference to us being underaged; regardless, Sid-The-Lid had no qualms in pulling off pints of draft ale for us at the weekends. We had found our watering hole.

If Mike didn't have bad luck, he'd have no luck at all. Sadly, Mike's grandfather also passed away that year. As a result of this, Mike found his grandad's old red Austin Metro parked at their home. Bizarrely, there was an antique air rifle tucked in the rear footwell that had gone unnoticed. For teenage kicks we'd rally the poor car round the hay and stubble fields that adjoined Mike's home, much to the farmer's indifference. We didn't damage the fields and he, like so many of an agricultural mindset, must have thought there were other much worse things that teenage boys could be doing; besides, we were his best fruit pickers and he wanted to keep us sweet. Roy would leave for work early in the morning and, so long as we parked the car in the exact same position each time, he was unaware of its newfound rallying pedigree.

Learning how to perform J-turns, handbrake turns and oversteering round stacks of bales was brilliant fun. Regrettably it all came to an abrupt end when Mike stoved the front end of the car into a solid gate post next to his house. The impact was sufficient to kill the engine. At the base of the gate post was a gigantic wasps' nest, about the size of a beach ball, and it was tightly woven through the hedge footing. The vexed wasps punished us as we pushed the car back to its parked position and we were both stung several times. We knew that the stings would be insignificant compared to Roy's wrath, so we had to think fast before he returned. We got the metro to its parked position and ran inside. Mike quickly thought of a plan and picked up the phone while I busily splashed vinegar on my wasp stings. Within an hour or so, the local scrap yard's recovery truck turned up to raise the dead Metro. Although he knew Roy would explode on his return to an empty driveway, Mike decided it would be better to pretend he sold the car to travellers and had no idea where it went, rather than Roy learning we had totalled it.

With the Metro gone, all we had to do to literally cover up our misdemeanour was to collect the headlight glass from the floor and kick fresh, dry dirt over the puddle of coolant. Preventing us from clearing up the crime scene was the cloud of wasps, still swarming angrily. I can't remember exactly who thought of it, but it was probably me – I had been stung the most and possessed a growing Special Forces wonderment. Regardless, we both agreed a *Who Dares Wins* approach would be the best way to eliminate the swarming wasps, and decided to make a Molotov cocktail to blow up the nest. Mike searched through his dad's garden shed and found two full cans of white grease aerosol spray, and cable tied them together. Next, we forced the cans into Mike's younger brother's school sports socks before heading back to the lawnmower shed where we went over the plan one final time. Mike would pour a bit of petrol out of the lawnmower onto the sock. I'd get in range of the nest, light the sock and throw it at the base of the gate. Mike would then shoot into the flames with his newly inherited air rifle and send the whole device skywards – burning all the wasps to a crisp – *Mazel Tov*!

I lit the end of the sports sock; a strong yellow flame went up and hot synthetic blims of sock dripped down. There was nothing for it than to run forward and throw the device at the foot of the gate post. It still remains the best throw I've ever made. The Molotov cocktail landed by the side of the nest and remained lit. The swarm now hummed at a terrific volume and it looked like the whole hedge was swaying. In a panic I ran back to the garden, jumped the wall next to where Mike was taking aim, yelling, *"SHOOT IT!"*

Unbeknown to us, or to Mike's father for that matter, the lady whom Roy had started courting was en route. In a bid to impress and win favour, she would occasionally drop in and surprise the family with fresh home-made quiches. It was really quite sweet, which made the whole incident that bit more regrettable. Mike and his siblings hadn't really warmed to her, not least because she used a dreadful-tasting wholemeal pastry mix as a base. Understandably so, in their eyes, she played second fiddle to their late mother.

Mike and I didn't hear or see her car approach from our firing position;

we were far too distracted. Nevertheless, at the split-second Mike pulled the trigger, she was driving just a few feet from the gate post. There was no uncertainty that Mike had hit his target. We heard the bang. We saw the mushroom cloud. We also learned the extreme volatility of white grease compressed in an aerosol form. The lady's car was pelted in shrapnel and flaming gloops of grease. If that wasn't enough of a shock, the next thing she saw from the other side of the blast zone was Mike, standing there holding a rifle. I remained hidden but did enough to peer over the wall. The lady must have mistakenly believed Mike had orchestrated a shock-and-awe ambush to ward her off. The car didn't stop and therefore we were given no chance to explain. She made a complete U-turn and drove away, never to be seen again by Mike or Roy.

There was a lot to be kept secret that day: we had taken out both the vicar and the terrorist.

The Major

My parents and Roy were not keen for Mike and me to drop out of education at 16 years old, despite the fact we both found it very tempting. I could have quite easily and happily found work as a gamekeeper, and I'm not sure that Mike's heart was in further education either. A compromise had to be found. Enrolling in a vocational course in the rural sector was the perfect solution. Newton Rigg College, Cumbria, offered up courses we were both interested in. Being gripped by rural pursuits, I chose to study Management of Game and Sporting Woodland, whereas Mike picked Countryside Management. In 1998 We crammed as much as we could into my Fiat Panda, left our childhoods behind in Shropshire and headed for the Lake District.

The College's residential accommodation left much to be desired. The only good thing to be found in the halls of residence was a fresh poster that caught Mike's eye. It read: *For Rent. East Wing of Newbiggin Hall. Would suit four students.* Mike ripped the poster down and that evening we drove to the hall with a couple of forestry students and secured the let. Newbiggin Hall was a Grade II listed building that dated back to the fifteenth century. A huge pad, built from red sandstone, it was both beautiful and iconic, with corniced stone chimneys and parapets. The owner was as eccentric as the Hall's heritage. He insisted we address him as 'Major'; his retired rank had been earned from an illustrious military career, mostly campaigns in the Congo, in Africa.

Newbiggin Hall, Cumbria. ©Dave Warren

"Look at the sun glistening on the hills there, it reminds me of Kili," the Major said to all four of us as he gestured west to the Pennine Hills. The hill range was just visible from our position up on the battlements. We admired the view, each holding a silver goblet of ale and wondering if the Pennines did indeed resemble Mount Kilimanjaro.

Ale was our payment for doing odd jobs on the estate. On one occasion we had finished clearing jackdaw nests from the chimneys of the parapets where the archers would once shelter and get warm. As we neared completion, the Major scuttled away and returned with our ale, which as usual was in silver goblets, carried on a silver tray. "We'll need these twigs gone if there's to be a civil war," the Major exclaimed. It turned out he wanted the hall to be battle ready, as he predicted hostilities between country folk and townsfolk. His way of life, he believed, would soon have to be fought for as the Labour government began tightening the screws on rural legislation. The Major decided he could use his new tenants' skills to his advantage and was keen to strike a deal. He gave us permission to collect firewood from any wind-snapped tree scattered across his estate; this would serve to tidy up his woods and fields. In exchange for filling the woodshed, he would allow us to shoot rabbit and pigeon, and fish the river that ran adjacent to the west wing.

The hall was imposing and cold. Other than a solid-fuel Aga in the kitchen, there was no central heating. Whilst we were excited to reside there, we knew we'd have to get busy to survive in some degree of comfort. On the first weekend, the foresters, buoyed with new-found freedom and hungry Husqvarna chainsaws, decided to practise felling wind-snapped trees in a nearby wood. For nostalgia's sake, Mike and I decided to cast a line in the Crowdundle Beck. The stream was a small, unassuming waterway not dissimilar to the River Onny, which ran a stone's throw from the hall. That morning, we dug up some worms and agreed to meet the guys in the late afternoon with the air rifles. The plan was to help log up the felled trees, then we'd all spread out and wait for the pigeons to roost. With a bit of luck we'd hit the pub on the way home and settle in front of the wood burner for a poacher's dinner. Heaven.

Mike and I walked just 50 metres upstream from the hall. We didn't have to walk too far before we found a stretch where the river slowed and a deep pool had been dug beneath a beech tree. The river wasn't at all wide. The opposite bank was in easy casting distance away, so we opted to freeline an earthworm in a bid to tempt a trout. No other kit was required. Simply the weight of the worm and the gentle current would hopefully be enough to get our bait onto the nose of a trout. Mike had first cast. "Yeah, I'm in, fish on!" Mike cried after he struck the rod and kept a tight line. The rod had quite a bend in it, much more than you'd expect for a small brook trout. Naturally, I thought he'd hooked a root of the beech tree and was simply being a bell-end. But then a silver flash pushed upstream from the root system, the tight line cut through the water towards some shallows and there we could make out the shape of a very handsome trout. I turned and sprinted back to the hall to get the landing net. The expected brook trout we hoped for would easily lift out of the water and onto the bank, however this unexpected beast was a much larger, sizable trout. If we were to stand any chance of getting it onto the bank, we'd need the net. Mike was still angling and playing the trout as I ran back to him. The trout tired, rolled over and came to the surface to be scooped up. Unbelievable – a rainbow trout of about 2 lbs, on the first cast! We moved upstream to the next pool. I had a couple of casts and trotted the worm downstream in time with the current, and bang! Another tight line and good bend in the rod. This time the trout showed himself with a leap out of the stream in a bid to shake the hook. I kept him honest and before too long we had our second sizable rainbow trout. These trout had no licence to be in this small waterway; it was obvious they must be escapees from a trout farm or stocked pond somewhere in the area. Believing there would only be a limited number of these beauties in the river, we elected not to fish any more and instead to take a walk further upstream and search for more likely hot spots.

Me and the Rainbow trout, Crowdundle Beck. ©Dave Warren

We were back at the hall in good time and gutted the fish. I decided to take the smaller of the two to the Major. His wife answered the door and took me through a passageway and into the drawing room to wait. The Major was amazed to receive the trout and was now of the belief he had the best trout river in the country. He made me swear to secrecy and to fish it only on the proviso I'd halve my catch with him each time. Of course, I agreed to his terms, so he shouted down to his wife to bring us two tankards of ale. While we had a celebratory drink, he walked me round the hall and showed me various spoils and Bushveld artefacts collected on his travels. Notable was a stuffed caiman in pride of place. This snappy fella was once shot by an ancestor and was being kept on display at Eton. To get him back to his rightful place in the family home, he was collected in the back of the Volvo – nose on the gear stick and tail sticking out of the boot.

Just before nightfall, Mike and I arrived at the wood to meet our housemates with the airguns. By the time we had stumbled up the timber track to meet the foresters, we had exhausted all our impressions of Rowley Birkin QC from *The Fast Show*, who seemed to have been inspired by our new landlord. We split some logs and filled the boot of the car, then returned to the hall an hour or so later in a car laden with logs, two rabbits and four pigeons. We could now fuel the log burner of the hall and the open fires we each had in our bedrooms. This was to be the *modus operandi* throughout our college course. On many occasions, our college lectures played second fiddle to the varying tasks deployed by the Major: fencing, firewooding, tree surgery, roof restoration and beating pheasants on his shoot days. This may have accounted for the dip in our grades. The hall and estate provided an immense bounty of game and dozens of large trout, which kept us all well fed. We learned to save the money our parents provided for a food allowance through buying veg in bulk from Penrith Market. The main consideration of this frugality was not to develop culinary prowess by cooking natural game dishes, but more so we could use our surplus at the pub. Mike was quick to get himself a Harris' hawk and trained it to hunt. Hawking added an extra string to our hunting bow, providing us with pheasant and an alluring distraction from the inconveniences of college. I soon became addicted to this artform – much favouring the hawk to the airgun.

Clarkey

Part of the college course required all students to undertake a lengthy period of industrial work experience. I secured a placement on a renowned sporting estate, Six Mile Bottom, Suffolk. The estate, approximately six miles to the south of Newmarket, was *the* most famous grey partridge manor in Britain from the turn of the 20th century to the inter-war period. In the decades following the Second World War, the ambition and ability to maintain such a prolific status were reduced in a series of events, concluding with the death of the owner, Lady Delamere, in 1986. Death duties and inheritance obligations fragmented the estate. In spite of the loss of acreage, reinstating the sporting grandeur and prestige was the sole ambition of the newly appointed Head Gamekeeper, Richard Clarke (Clarkey or Click to his friends) when he took on the sporting obligations of a much-reduced 12,000 acres of the original boundary.

I arrived at Six Mile Bottom for a 16-week unpaid work placement in the summer of 1998, aged 17, during my first year of college. I was sad to leave the lads and stately home behind, but equally excited for a new adventure that would only be for four months. I was polite, honest, doing well academically, took instruction well and knew the importance of a firm handshake. I arrived at Six Mile Bottom in the late afternoon. I thought turning up in plenty of time and being ready to start the next morning would win favour. I was a young buck, rather full of it having just passed my driving test, and smugly rattled down Clarkey's driveway in my Fiat Panda. My bravado was immediately called into check at the point of pulling into the courtyard. In front of Richard's house was a surround of some 20 kennels and an array of spaniels, cockers, terriers and labradors, all of whom rushed to the front of their runs. None-more-curious to see who was stepping out of the car were the dogs residing in kennels one, two and three, nearest to the porch. They were Max, Bob and Zen; three huge German Shepherds who intimidated equally in temper and form. I knocked on the door, and as it opened, I found myself standing in front of Richard Clarke. He was a big man, well built and some 6 foot 4 tall. He sported a shaved head and tattoos on his arms that showed from under his rolled-up sleeves. He had a presence that immediately commanded respect, in a metre, voice and tone akin to notorious gangster Lenny McLean, which was appropriate, as he was now my 'Guvnor'.

"You made it then. If you want to be here tomorrow, you need to go and get a haircut." Clarkey pulled a bundle of cash from his pocket and handed me £10. This transaction served to affirm Richard's authority and establish his leadership style on a firm footing from the outset. He had no time for scruffy-haired louts on his watch. I got a haircut and was subsequently plunged into a whirlwind of gamekeeping obligations. From day 1, the more I worked alongside Richard, the harder I wanted to work for him. His personal resolve to return the estate to its famous past took formidable determination and guts. No one worked harder than Click, and he was a solid influence. Not only was there woodland to restore and margin habitat to re-claim from intensive arable practice, but the region was plagued by poaching, rural crime and illegal hare coursing. Richard had to stamp this out in order to make a success of it and protect all that was his. I had arrived a decade into his mission. I was very green, but soon – from working on the ground – I was losing weight, gaining muscle, and in receipt of life lessons unobtainable from higher education.

*****

Breeding, training and developing a decent longdog (lurcher/greyhound/ deerhound) is an acquired skill. Showcasing the attributes of a longdog, off the track, has traditionally been done by setting it against the formidably fit and evasive brown hare so that he exhibits his best characteristics in a bid to catch his quarry. By pitting two dogs against the same hare, you will be able to decipher which one is better able to course the hare by marking each dog against the following criteria. **The Value of Speed**: to keep or regain pace in order to match the hare's ability to evade, but under no circumstance can speed without subsequent work be allowed to decide a course. **The Go-Bye**: being a clear length behind his opponent, the trailing dog passes him in a straight run and gets a clear length ahead of him. **The Turn**: turning the hare beyond a 90-degree angle from her previous line as a result of pressure from the greyhound. **The Wrench**: turning the hare less than a 90-degree angle by pressure from the greyhound. **The Merit of a Kill**: the way in which the greyhound collects the hare, by his own merit or the actions of his competitor. **The Trip**: throwing the hare off her legs but not resulting in a kill.

Six Mile Bottom is steeped in hare coursing heritage. The rich, chalky, clay loam soil and huge arable fields in the region provide an incredibly alluring and beneficial running canvas on which to train a greyhound. The ground is quick draining, forgiving on the cruciate tendon, yet firm enough for the dog to endure and sustain a long gait to tire the hare. Greyhound and lurcher owners would travel miles, particularly out of Walthamstow and other London suburbs, up the M11, to train and hunt on the firm-going ground. As a consequence of Richard's successful efforts to reduce the fox population, the hares returned in good numbers, which in turn drew the coursers who expected free rein over the fields. Hare coursing has been a sport and pastime of both noblemen and laymen since 150AD. However, the people who were practising illegal hare coursing on Richard's beat were most certainly some very nasty characters.

✎©April Coppini

"The first rule of you being here: for fuck's sake – you *DO NOT* get yourself involved with coursers. If you approach them in the truck and they think you're me, they're gonna fucking try to kill you. That's why Max, Bob and Zen are here." Richard was serious. Unbeknown to me, he believed there was a contract on his life after implementing a zero-tolerance policy on illegal hare coursing for the 10 years prior to my arrival. His vigilante measures were courageous. Richard and his gamekeepers had spoiled many contentious courses on which huge wagers were placed. His resolve and stance served to change the situation beyond the police's ambition or ability to uphold the law and crack down on rural crime. It was a bold, fierce and an aggressive bid to protect his manor and it gained him a ferocious reputation.

On my first morning, Richard introduced me to his German Shepherds, Max, Bob and Zen. I was instructed to never let them out of the kennel without him, not that I had any inclination to do so! Max and Bob came from a trainer based at Dartmoor Prison, and Zen from the Cambridgeshire Police. These three Shepherds were just shy of making the assessed grade and unless an appropriate home was found, would have been destroyed. Max specialised in doing short work in the corridors and cells of the prison and was particularly loyal and stayed close. Zen and Bob were athletic and excelled in escape work; they both specialised in tracking and immobilising fleeing perpetrators at range. Between them, and with Richard's own methods of dissuading hare coursers, Six Mile Bottom became a troublesome venue for coursers to slip longdogs.

A spoilt course, on which vast amounts of cash or debt had been laid down between top-grade greyhounds, is beyond frustrating for the vested parties. More so is having to run from a German Shepherd at full throttle, losing your top greyhound, driving home in a vehicle void of windows or on seats filled with dog mess and deer gralloch, or having your vehicle spiked with a bail spike. These are all inconveniences that perhaps would dissuade you from revisiting the region. Worryingly for me, given the backgrounds of some coursing enthusiasts, the possibility of serious revenge and reprisal was a constant and very real threat, so being vigilant and never leaving yourself vulnerable was the uppermost consideration among the keepers. "Max never leaves my side, Bob stays in the truck so they don't nick my motor and Zen gets to go for a jolly every now and then – nowadays they usually disappear as soon as I get out the motor and line the dogs up next to me," Richard explained.

Clarkey, Zen, Bob and Max ©Richard Clarke

Richard was tough and brave beyond rational consideration, an alpha male with mental resolve that demanded excellence. He did the best he could with what he had and would not suffer laziness or stupidity. When working for Richard, the days were always long and your excuses for not *yet* completing tasks were insignificant. You either had to work faster or later (if you fell behind) – a far cry from the luxury I enjoyed of mooching at leisure on the Newbiggin Estate. With that said, Richard was always fair in his expectations, and the fact that he had been there and done it all in his formative years meant he would only set tasks that were achievable, if ambitious. If you genuinely struggled or needed help, he would weigh in and see the job through; but, if you were being a bit pathetic, the responsibility was squarely on your shoulders to achieve your goals and manage your time.

My likening of Clarkey to the mighty Lenny McLean for his mannerisms, voice and tone was also somewhat era-appropriate, as – on one occasion – Guy Richie, Brad Pitt and other cast members of the film *Snatch* descended on the infamous estate to submerge themselves in its heritage and film the hare coursing part of the movie. Clarkey's good friend Vinnie Jones literally brought a Hollywood culture to his doorstep, which boosted the ambition and pride of the squad of keepers on the estate.

Each Sunday, a squad of rum-cove-gentlemen would spew from a cortege of vans and pick-ups into Richard's courtyard. These chaps were fondly known as the London Boys. Richard's London boys consisted of roofers, joiners, builders, varying tradesmen and the occasional cockney wide-boy who would travel up from the 'smoke', breakfast at the local truck stop, then arrive in Six Mile Bottom. Each *geezer* would do half a day's work for Clarkey amid endless banter, then be driven out across the estate to various pigeon hides constructed by the gamekeepers and enjoy a full afternoon's pigeon shooting as their reward. This relationship served everybody well. The farmers would receive crop protection, the London Boys had a great away day, and Clarkey would get his sheds re-felted and his workshop stocked with all sorts of fixings, fastenings and tools that *fell off lorries'* in and around central London. Should any hare coursers turn up, there was plenty of muscle on tap to dissuade illegal activity. As you would expect, the kit and spare fixings were shelved neatly and the workbench was always immaculate.

"What's that old shitty trainer doing up there?" I asked, pointing to an out-of-place, torn, muddied trainer, probably a size 10, hanging in what seemed to be pride of place (but which looked so out of place above the clean work bench).

"It's one of Zen's trophies. Have you been down to the Studs yet?" Richard smiled as he replied, holding the lone sports trainer. The Studs was an area of arable ground surrounded by the traditional equine stud fencing that was common about Newmarket. The boundary consisted of a post-and-rail fence line. The horizontal rails were 6-inch ship-lap timber boards, spaced with about a 1-foot gap between them to a height of about 5 feet, all creosoted to a dark brown finish. Behind the stud fence was a thick, stock-proof hedge, typically planted up with holly, hawthorn, buckthorn and blackthorn. He then went on to explain the significance of the reference.

"We spotted this bloke hare coursing on the Studs. He was right at the far end, walking back to his Subaru, which he'd tried to hide on the other side of the fence. As soon as he clocked me, he legged it. Zen jumped over me and was out through the driver's window after him like a fucking land shark. This bloke was trying to run, but the ground was soft so he was falling over in panic. With Zen closing in on him, all the London Boys were cheering Zen – go on boy – fucking brilliant! Anyway, Zen was gaining on him, he was never going to make the gate and get round to his motor. So, to get out of the Stud, the lad took a dive through the rails. Well, I'll never forget the screams when he got cut up with all them thorns. He was stuck there knowing Zen was just about to tear him a new jam roll[1]. The noise that came from his north[2] was so harrowing… I called Zen off. But Zen couldn't resist having a sniff of this bloke who was wailing and covered in claret. The bloke was trying to pull himself through a thorn hedge. I called Zen again, but before he come back, he only went and ripped the bloke's fucking trainer off his foot and brought it back to me. Zen was pleased as punch, tail up and peacocking all the way back up the Studs, full swagger, right back to the truck, with this trainer in his mouth. Well, the London Boys were on the floor, what a bubble[3]. We went down and taxed his motor of loose change. While we were doing that, the lad hobbled up to us in tears, covered in claret and begged me to give him a £1 back so he could get home over the Dartford Crossing. Well, that's the only time I felt sorry for one of them, so I gave him a pound, but Zen kept his trainer. Fuck we're hard on 'em - I can't believe I'm still alive.

---

1. Jam roll = arsehole.
2. North south = mouth.
3. Bubble bath = laugh.

There isn't much let-up in a gamekeeper's diary. The fact that game shooting is seasonal means you would expect it to have natural end points for tasks, but in reality they all merge as there is much to be done between the seasons. You are either busy, or busy preparing to be busy. There is never a time when machinery can't be cleaned, fixed, maintained, habitat developed and predators controlled. After completing my priorities, such as setting up pheasant-laying pens, collecting eggs, incubating, setting up the rearing field, hatching, rearing, setting up release pens and releasing poults, I fell back on a list of preparatory work, readying for the next phase or project to satisfy Click's enterprising mindset. At 17 years of age it was good for me to have this influence, and it certainly instilled a sense of pride and an ambitious work ethic.

In the back of the motor ©Richard Clarke

Ralph Brown

It was a natural transition for Mike and I to go from a rural college to an agricultural university. Happily, there was none finer in the country than Harper Adams Agricultural College, located in our home county of Shropshire. Mike and I both got onto degree courses and moved back to the 'shire.

We both graduated in 2004, still uncertain how to utilise our Bachelor of Science degrees. Mike's was in Land-Based Industries. Mine was in Rural Enterprise and Land Management. Chartered surveying didn't whet my whistle, so I stayed in Shropshire, odd-jobbing. Mike was adamant he wanted to live in Scotland. As a child he always dug out Scottish landscape photography books from the school library and imagined himself exploring upland ranges, immersing himself in the wilderness and embracing the weather and serenity. Being a little braver and bolder than me, Mike chose to take a punt and settled in Perthshire, central Scotland. The transition was everything he'd hoped it would be – so much so that he spent a good deal of time persuading me to follow suit. Trusting Mike's word, I loaded my trusty German shorthaired pointer (GSP), Ralph Brown, into my car and followed Mike north of the border.

Ralph Brown and I had been inseparable since the day I'd bought him. It was during the spring of 2004, my final year of university, when I got talking to a local man called Dave Whittingham. He invited me to watch his goshawk hunt, not too far from the university grounds. Providing the slips for his goshawk was his impressive German shorthaired pointer named Hearty. At the end of a successful day in the field, Whittingham invited me back to his pub in Telford for a pint of Guinness. "If you liked Hearty, you'll love this lad. He's the last of his litter," he said as he plonked the sweetest 8-week-old GSP puppy on the table next to my Guinness. As soon as I looked at him I knew his name and that I'd be taking him home that day. "It's Ralph Brown!" I announced, as if I'd known this pup all my life. Ralph vied for my attention and enjoyed a fuss. Licking Guinness off my fingers was his new favourite treat. I was unable to look past him or leave him, so I placed him in a box on the front seat of my car, and we began our life adventures.

Having gleaned the fundamentals of raptor husbandry from Mike, I chanced my arm moving to Scotland in 2005 and found work in flying demonstrations, spending four years developing a squad of raptors at Blair Drummond Safari Park, just outside Stirling. It was a small, modest team of raptors, yet, in their day, they were world-class. A huge female white-tailed sea eagle I named 'Snatch' and a lanneret (male lanner falcon) named 'Growler' (I was young, OK?) were the stars of my demonstration team. It took some convincing to get the Safari Park to buy Snatch. I wanted an extravaganza and felt that a 5-kilo eagle with a wingspan of over two metres would add huge kudos and be the showstopper of my displays. No other collection in the country was flying this iconic native eagle. Maybe it was their purchase price, or their tendency to be a bit bitey towards their handler that put so many off. Snatch had cost £3,500, more than I had ever spent on anything in my life. It was ridiculous to think I was flying something nearly four times the value of my car (and probably the combined value of everything I owned) with only very basic tracking equipment. Nevertheless, the faith shown by my employers paid off, and with much excited trepidation 'Snatch' flew regularly throughout the display seasons in all conditions. She would speck-out into the clouds, beyond the naked eye, and stoop hard for a floating fish lure I'd throw into the loch that backed the display ground. It created a phenomenal aesthetic that is hard to describe but always wowed the crowd and won me huge favour with the park owners.

Me and Snatch ~ 2002 📷©Neil Aldridge

It was a privileged opportunity to train and fly a variety of iconic raptors, but being immersed in the world of 'flying displays' as a professional trainer/presenter/flying demonstrator (call it what you will) inhibited the celestial fanaticism that burned deep within me to practise falconry in its purest from – hunting wild game (*quarry*) with a trained bird of prey, as I had done so fondly with Mike at Newbiggin Hall. At first, I had been excited to introduce expectant tourists to the world of raptors and present to them my immaculately-turned-out hawks. However, as years three and four rolled past, the neatly mown lawn of the flying arena proved to be a bland postage stamp on which to fly hawks, void of the features that make casting a hawk into the air exciting. Here, there was no fieldcraft, no pitting of wits against the elements and terrain, or the sensation of the presence of a natural quarry. There was little to be gained in fine tuning appetite and condition or in capturing instinctive behaviour simply for the hawk to be denied the opportunity to satisfy her natural hunting instincts or fly to the limit of her ability pursuing an evasive quarry. I felt discontented to practise this lesser artform and resented the unavoidable intrusion of an audience. I yearned for splendid solitude and to return to a life away from tourists. At that time I realised something that will sound quite strange – I missed feeling hungry. That may be idiotic to say, but the excitement of hunting for sustenance when hungry, as was often the case at Newbiggin Hall, provided a thrilling impetus to flying a hawk. Senses heighten, decisions become critical, and the desire for my hawk to grasp rabbit or pheasant compelling. It was a far cry from the flavourless flying arena.

It was the end of my fifth season of flying demonstrations. Each year I'd orchestrated some 650 flying displays for about 350,000 visitors. I was pleased that so many people had experienced these beautiful birds, but I needed a change and was at a crossroads. I had such fond memories of the Six Mile Bottom Estate that I wanted to fall back and be the familiar lone working gamekeeper – a life that I was content to live in the late 1990s. After a quick phone call to Clarkey, I managed to secure some part-time work back on the estate. I knew Ralph Brown would have more stimulation there and, now in my late 20s, I was keen to find work that would reward me beyond a display falconer's pay cap. I packed all I could into the boot of the car and, sensing a new beginning, Ralph Brown jumped onto the front seat and we drove south to Suffolk.

Richard still had game-shooting obligations, but on a much smaller farm of 2,500 acres that once formed part of the original estate. He was in the formative stages of setting up a simulated game-shooting enterprise on this land, and there was plenty to be done in formulating a clay pigeon shooting ground. I knew Richard would be competitive and hungry for success, and being a part of the expected hustle suited my desire for change. It was great to be back at Six Mile Bottom some ten years later. I took a day or two to familiarise myself with the woodlands and drives, as well as being kept busy by an expectant boss as Clarkey showed me around the new clay pigeon enterprise and newly relocated workshop. Although I had been away for 10 years, and had become fully independent and mature, under Clarkey's governance it was impossible not to still feel tiny.

"What, no trainer?" I asked Clarkey with a smile on my face, as we returned to the original spot where the unfortunate guy's shoe had hung. "The wild west days are over, it all came to a head in 2004," he said, looking visibly relieved.

It transpired that during my absence a young lad named Fred Moss had been shot, cut into a number of pieces, bagged up, then burned on a pile of wooden pallets on a nearby estate. On the afternoon of Fred's disappearance, his parting words on leaving his home were apparently that he was off hare coursing. When Moss didn't return, his friends and family descended on various hare-rich venues across the country to look for him. Of course, Clarkey was a prime suspect.

"They all turned up here, and they all thought I'd fucking killed Fred Moss," Clarkey exclaimed. "They said they wanted to go through my sheds to look for the body, but I thought they wanted to get me in a shed to hang me. I had Max, Zen and Bob all lined up next to me on the yard, and that's how I managed to level with Fred's brother." He went on to explain that he took a few of the search party to look around his sheds. Realising there was no body and Clarkey was innocent of any involvement, phone numbers were exchanged and Clarkey promised to get all of the keepers across the farms of East Anglia to go through their buildings and look out for Fred, his vehicle, anything! Satisfied at that, the group left, onto the next farm in search of Fred. "After that it all calmed down. Thank God. With all the aggro, in them days I thought I'd never see fifty."

It transpired that the interaction between Clarkey and friends of the Moss family brokered a new dawn of mutual respect for each other. The animosities were dialled down. Richard found incidences of poaching reduced and that maintaining his gung-ho response was no longer appropriate or necessary, much to everyone's relief. "Anyway, that's all in the past. It's Sandringham tomorrow – we're off to see my mate Dave Clark and do a little job for the Royals. For fuck's sake, iron a shirt and wear a tie," Clarkey said as he walked off and busied himself.

The simulated game enterprise was certainly less gritty and hard fought than the pheasant-shooting side of the operation. Richard Clarke's brand, Six Mile Bottom Shoot, was beginning to take off. One of my first gigs was to load up the clay trailer and accompany Richard to Sandringham Estate. We provided some entertainment for the Royals. Watching the two princes shoot clays and enjoy themselves was a far cry from having catapult-wielding hare coursers slingshot ball bearings at you!

In spite of this newfound, relaxed atmosphere, Clarkey never lost his expectations of my work rate. 'Where are you?' or 'How's it looking?' were questions I could expect at any point of the day or night. This provided little opportunity to do anything other than gamekeeping or sleeping. In what little spare time I had, I hawked alone. Clarkey gave me permission to slip my bay-winged hawk at rabbits that proliferated in the shelter belts and hedgerows of the famed estate. I was an unknown falconer to the local hawkers and, given my ambitions to remain undiscovered, was quite purposeful not to seek or befriend any local falconers or join the regional falconry clubs. I caught plenty of rabbits and pheasants for the pot, and was glad to have gained distance and find solitude to continue my passion once more.

A couple of years rolled by. February marked the end of another season, so I stood my hawk down for a well-deserved moult. She had kept me well fed and had earned her down-time as I continued with the springtime duties on the estate. One such event was the 2010 Kennel Club Pointer and Setter Trial. I was to be the steward of the beat, spending two days guiding the expectant gallery of trial enthusiasts, onlookers, competitors and electrified pointing dogs across the vast swathes of quarter-grown winter wheat that characterises the desertification of East Anglia.

On the first morning, amid all the general confusion and yapping, one of the judges took me aside and, with a familiar prequel set to make me cringe, said: "I want to introduce you to someone. You'll like this guy, he's a falconer."

*****

PART 2:

PEREGRINES OVER POINTERS

Devolamus ut iterum sublimemus
We stoop to soar again

Stuart Fall

Thus I was introduced to Stuart Fall – a tall, strong, broad, rangy man closely resembling a mop-haired Billy Connolly. Stu was dressed in a smart Tattersall shirt and green tweed waistcoat. He held a hand-rolled cigarette and was distracted by the laughter and camaraderie amongst the trialers. Through gritted teeth I made polite conversation after Stu came forward to say hello. He seemed such a big presence in the gallery I feared he was too pretentious for my liking, so I made my excuses to disappear back to my truck. Stuffing a handful of shotgun cartridges in my pocket, I headed forth with the judges to find the next Field Trial Champion.

Lunchtime came around, and while the judges deliberated on which dogs were worthy of the next round, all I had for sustenance was a warm can of Guinness that had spent the last few days rolling around in the boot of the truck. Blowing the grit and wiping the pheasant (or maybe rabbit) blood off the lid, I cracked the can open and supped. Stu emerged once more and offered up some scotch eggs. Survival instincts took over and I decided to endure the likely far-fetched falconry drivel such that I could keep dipping into his luncheon basket. Surprisingly, the conversation steered away from hawking as Stu explained he was here to catch up with his friends on the trialling circuit and to see his line of pointer dogs run. He took time away from the rest of the group to go into more detail about his breeding, the qualities required of a field trial winner, and more so, why it was important to get pointers to run to a trial standard under a falcon. I felt bad at having been so sceptical because I soon realised that I liked this guy. I left the meet at the end of the day feeling like I had gained a valuable insight into the field trial world, and was glad to see some top trainers run their pointers. I returned to my truck and put the shotgun back in its sleeve.

"What are you doing tonight?" Stu asked.

"Err... not much," I replied, which was all the information Stu needed to invite me round for supper. Within a few hours I was sitting in Stu's kitchen and was the grateful recipient of an enormous roast chicken dinner. The centrepiece of the table was a huge baking tray of roast potatoes, perfectly cooked in duck fat. The delicious food was complemented by an evening of engaging storytelling and a gut full of wine. Stu's kitchen was the engine room of the house. Not only did all the entertaining happen here, but it was also his library, his workshop, and the space in which he found most comfort. It was inviting, reverberant with laughter, homely, unapologetic, bold and considered. It was Stu.

The brightest spark to radiate through this setting was Mandy, Stu's wife (known more fondly as Manders or Mands). From the outset, Mands was unable to disguise her two superpowers: (i) making you howl with laughter, and (ii) making you feel loved and cared for. Manders possessed a fantastic memory and would glide in and out of conversations with impressive facts, anecdotes, quirky details and rib-ticklingly blasphemous expletives that served to lighten up any yarn – you couldn't help but instantly love her and her outlandish sense of humour. In spite of the compelling conversation, I found it impossible to refrain from casting an eye across to Stu's extensive book collection. Some alluring titles caught my eye: *Gamehawk, A Merlin For Me, Gamehawking At Its Very Best, A Bird In The Hand, A Rage For Falcons, Merlins Of The Wicklow Mountains, The Pointer, The Flying of Falcons, D'Arcussia's Falconry 1643, A Perfect Booke For Keeping Sparhawkes, The Modern Falconer, Hood Leash and Lure, The Pointer and His Predecessors, As The Falcon Her Bells, The Lure of the Falcon, A Manual of Falconry, Kings and their Hawks, The Hound and the Hawk.* These were just a few of the books on the top shelf; there were dozens more.

I'd never seen so many falconry books. There were titles I'd never heard of, covering varying styles of falconry throughout the world and over the centuries. For each book, Stu would have a fun story of how he came by it, who sold it to him and where. Like Mands, he had an incredible memory. He'd pull various titles from the shelf and unashamedly open the cover to reveal a personalised dedication and signature from the author, or signatures of the falconers with whom he had hawked. "What's your favourite, Stu?" Not being very well read, I was curious to discover a title I might like. Stu then lifted a brown envelope off the shelf. I forget what he said, possibly nothing at all, but I instantly recognised the look of a man in the full state of enamoured pride, exactly as I had first witnessed some 19 years earlier when Roy watched Mike fly his kestrel. Stu slowly pulled at the envelope's seal and withdrew a wodge of A4 writing paper. On the well-thumbed paper was scrawled biro. It was the original, handwritten draft of Helen Macdonald's *H is for Hawk*. I recognised the reverence with which he unveiled it, but naively, not having read the book or having known Stu for very long, I wasn't quite sure why he cherished it so. No doubt I'd tease it out of him later.

When my attention wasn't fixed to the bookshelf, it was drawn to the vast array of falcon hoods Stu used and had collected over the years. His was a substantial collection, all individually pinned to the wall of his kitchen by long carpet tacks. Some were heavily dusted, a few recently used, yet the substantial collection took into account all the different beak shapes and skull sizes of their intended recipients. Lined up, they were ready to be selected and slipped onto a falcon at a moment's notice. As we sat beneath them, he reached up and passed a few of them down. "Pineo's are the best," Stu said as he handed to me a few examples of American hoodmaker Doug Pineo's hoods to look at. "I bought these hoods off Doug at the falconry fair along with my hawking vest – though the right pocket of my vest is fucked. The ferrets bit their way out in my goshawking days."

The Hood

Hoods of some sort or another have been placed on the heads of falcons ever since these raptors were first tamed and used for hunting some 4,000 years ago in the Far East, before spreading westwards into Europe sometime around 560 AD. The hood blindfolds the falcon, preventing her from receiving visual stimuli that may trigger her natural escape reflex. In the hood, with eyes covered, she will remain standing, and be highly unlikely to flail her wings (an action known as bating).

An ill-fitting hood will incite scratching and bating as the falcon attempts to rid herself of the irritant. Poorly fitting hoods may rub the falcon's eyelids, bruise the cere (the skin that surrounds the nostrils at the base of the beak), and can trigger a gagging reflex resulting in an absolute welfare disaster. It really takes an educated eye to ensure that the hood is correct for the falcon. This is why most falconers have extensive hood collections.

To leave a falcon in a hood unnecessarily is very bad practice. It is the responsibility of the falconer to diminish her reaction to stimuli that would ordinarily cause alarm, enabling her to remain in a relaxed state when exposed to the usual events of a home environment – turning the falcon from escapologist to contented observer. Use of the hood enables the falconer to do this in gradual increments and reduces the risk of trauma.

The conversation moved away from goshawks and on to the peregrine falcon. Stu continued chatting as I examined the delicate and intricate stitching of the Pineo hood. "You know you've made it in falconry when you walk onto the moor, unhood your peregrine and watch her eat up the sky without skipping a wingbeat," Stu said. "After she's left the fist, you should be able to roll a cigarette, and by the time you've finished smoking it, look up and see her at a grand, ready to stoop the grouse marked down by your pointer."

Stu paused. He looked with fondness across the room at his English pointers – Jess, Sham and Cody – curled up on their bed, probably remembering a time when their gallant efforts in finding elusive game birds secured a point and gave him the opportunity to cast his falcon into the wind. With a wry smile, and without averting his gaze from his dogs, Stu finished rolling his cigarette, licked the paper, rolled his big thumb over the lighter wheel and drew. He then held a long exhale without ever losing the smile on his face – he was dreaming of pointers flushing quarry and falcons stooping from the heavens.

Smoking hand-rolled cigarettes embodied Stu's demeanour. Each cigarette he smoked was complemented by the natural ebb and flow of his prudent personality. It was something I noticed while we sat in his kitchen as he listened attentively to my life story. In Stu's company, smoking didn't seem repulsive, dirty or disgusting. Smoking, dare I say it, suited Stu. His rolling tobacco had a familiar, approachable, musky smell to it. It was recognisable – like wax jackets and gunpowder – and was not at all objectionable. For Stu, a naturally kind and forbearing man, drawing on a lit cigarette was something he did when he exercised his patience, making allowances for someone's exuberant and eager waffling, mine in particular. It was something he did when he needed time to consider and reflect on situations or devise a remedial approach. It was something he did when he recognised you needed to be put at ease. Stu was incredibly humorous and would laugh at life's absurdities. More often than not, he'd have some quip ready to offer. Smoking gave him the opportunity to lay in wait for a chance to say something witty, but also something sincere, reassuring or loving when it was dearly needed. The best moments were when he exhaled like the sputtering exhaust of a misfiring generator, and, from behind the intermittent smoke screen, you'd see Stu's beaming face, eyes watering, uncontrollably laughing at one of his own jokes.

Grand or 1,000 feet was Stu's (and most UK falconers') acceptable altitude pitch from which a falcon should turn over and stoop her quarry. At that altitude, should the quarry be flushed or pass directly beneath her, she will fold so that the tips of the outermost primary flight feathers on her wings touch the tips of her tail feathers. She holds this position in a perfect beak-first, tombstone dive, until she quickens her talons to the flesh of her quarry, either raking through or grasping her prey. *Two grand* is an exceptional pitch, and rarely witnessed in the UK lowlands. Comparatively small field sizes limits the distance from which game can foray from cover and, as such, restricts the altitude some falconers will push for, simply because the quarry would make cover before the falcon could descend from such a height. However, on 3,000+ acres of open moorland, the aesthetic of a *two grand* stoop is very much achievable and witnessing such a dive will leave you astounded. How fast a falcon travels in the stoop remains contentious. We know through scientific experiment that the peregrine has been calculated to stoop at speeds up to 240 mph. However, thanks to readily available, real-time trackers, we know it is typically between 100-150 mph. A more insightful answer to the question was given by renowned falconer Diana Durman-Walters when, after a successful outing hawking duck with her peregrine, her jubilant and suitably impressed apprentice asked, "How fast was she going when she killed that?" Cooly, Diana answered, "Enough – she was going fast enough."

Stu needed no invitation to regale me with intricate and romantic details of flights he had orchestrated throughout his lifetime. "When the quarry flushes – when that tiny flickering black dot waiting on in the clear blue sky puts in a stoop – she accelerates so fast that at first she becomes invisible to the naked eye. Your eyes can't keep up with her. Then she gets closer and you pick her up again, a faint black streak heading for the horizon. The only noise you hear is the wind screaming through her bells, until she rakes, then it's a big fucking crump as the pheasant bounces off the frozen stubbles." Stu was unable to contain himself. He continued sharing his stories long into the night. My heart was racing as I dreamt of stoops and rakes while camped out on Stu's sofa, squished between his three pointers.

Two days later, Stu and I spent an evening hunting with his male merlin, known as a Jack. Jack merlins are small falcons. Without feathers you could fit one in a half-pint glass. Owing to their dexterity and speed of flight, merlins primarily specialise in feeding on song birds and other small passerines. Stu decided to use one of his steadiest and oldest bitches, Jess, to systematically quarter over the low-cut stubble on one of my beats on Six Mile Bottom in search of passerines. Jess was Stu's semi-retired English pointer. She was entering the autumn of her life and was an old hand at this pointing malarkey. Jess was very biddable and sensitive to finding skylarks near to where we walked. A younger, sprightlier pointer would likely range wider at terrific pace and flush quarry beyond the sprint range of the merlin. Also, the exuberant carriage of a pacey pointer would likely run through the delicate scent of such tiny European passerines as they lay hidden in the stubble. It is far better for the merlin to preside over a steady pointer, one that intricately hunts closer to heel in steady, shallow beats. On detecting the scent of the game – larks in this instance – the pointer will naturally freeze, remain motionless and lock its body length perfectly in line with the quarry. Then, on command, the pointer is released from this set position and sent in to flush.

Stu was a joiner by trade, and his hands were like shovels, hardened by years of constructing oak timber frames. On his bare fist perched a tiny 200-gram merlin. Each delicate talon of this micro falcon found purchase by gripping the cracked skin canyons of Stu's thumb and index finger. On each leg of the merlin were delicate leather straps, held fast between Stu's huge carpenter's fingers. "She knows what we're after," Stu said, as he let Jess out of the van and began walking ahead of me. I kept pace with Stu as his long gate marched into the field. I was instantly transported back to my youth, bumbling behind Reverend Payne.

Stu's long, curly, windswept hair acted as a sail and kept us straight as we bored into the breeze. His head continued to turn slowly from our left flank back to our right. He fixated on Jess bisecting our path as she ran a beautiful quartering pattern, hunting for larks upwind of us. On occasion Stu would peep his whistle to stop Jess. Obligingly, she'd stop then turn to look at him. Using his empty right hand to signal direction, Stu would conduct Jess, sending her into likely hotspots – patches of taller stubble created by the combine harvester lurching on uneven ground, for example. As she worked on, Stu continued to dote on Jess, introducing me to the term "LBJ", or "little brown job" – the acronym he used to group all small, ground-dwelling birds found in late-summer stubble, mostly skylarks, thrushes and meadow pipits. "If Jess sees me carrying a merlin, she stops on every LBJ in the field. If I'm carrying the peregrine she won't stop unless she's on a partridge or pheasant. When I had the goshawk, she kept out of the fields and hunted through the thicket for rabbits. She's a thinker."

It took a while but eventually Jess snapped onto point, indicating there was an LBJ lying clamped ahead of us ('clamping' being the term used to describe prey that are lying flat and hoping the danger will pass). We levelled with the frozen pointer and got within the merlin's sprint range, then Stu clicked his fingers. Each click served as a release command, triggering Jess to move forward on the scent. The feeling of being behind the pointer at this moment is akin to winding a jack-in-the-box toy. You are gripped by absorbing, excruciating tension and compelled to continue clicking in anticipation until the flush. A lark burst from the stubble. My reaction was to startle at the flashing wings that launched from our golden plane. Meanwhile, the young merlin's reaction was instantaneous – he dived forward from Stu's fist and engaged in a tail chase. Before I'd steadied myself, the merlin had set about pursuing the lark, and the pair were about 30 metres away. The merlin stayed on the lark's tail as it jinked and swerved, attempting to throw the merlin off course. I was at a loss to predict what was going to happen next; I was simply compelled to watch, transfixed as this zipping course was traced in the sky before me. Unable to gain a commanding lead from the merlin, the lark then pulled up sharply and began to ring over a large stand of conifers known as the Vicarage Drive, with the merlin tenaciously questing behind. Not capable of matching the fitness of the lark over a duration of about a minute, the merlin was found wanting and forced to concede the loss. He stooped down, empty taloned, to rest on a fence post, leaving me standing in awe at what we had just witnessed.

The cries of the skylark were not something I'd ever heard before. The calls were not alarmist or panicked as you might expect from something that had been pursued by such a capable predator. No, this was the call of a skylark that was gladly mocking the beaten merlin. She sang her heart out with indignation, sarcastically goading her resting enemy and letting those in earshot know she was victorious. Point made, she flew off into the distance, leaving the Cambridgeshire countryside ghostly silent.

©April Coppini

My connection with Stu grew strong. We became pretty inseparable in the field, and he naturally assumed the position of my falconry mentor. In doing so, he opened his home to me. The warmth with which he and Mandy greeted me, or any visitor, was equalled only by the kettle, which remained in constant use. A mix of tea, coffee, rolling tobacco and incense sticks filled the air. The eagle-eyed pointers were always ready to spot whenever a mug or cigarette was absent from hand, and they took it as an invitation to nose-nuzzle in for fuss and attention. I loved it there.

Each time I sat in Stu's kitchen I would draw down books from his falconry collection and flick through the pages as he recalled endless anecdotes from the field. The more we talked about gamehawking, the more we concurred and began to define our preferred art form – a traditional, purist notion. We were adamant that we wanted to get onto the moors and try our best to orchestrate the fastest natural sporting phenomenon – the fastest predator in the world vying to catch one of the fastest and most capable escapologists of any quarry species: the red grouse. It was here that our quest for *Peregrines over Pointers* was born.

We decided that this discipline of falconry was the pinnacle, considering each and every aspect. **The grouse**: fast, wild, alert, fit, and more than capable of evading capture in its natural habitat. **The peregrine**: pure, tenacious in ambition and authentic in all her facets. **The pointer**: athletic, hearty, quartering the moor at pace with extended gait, running flat casts and knowingly working for the falconer with self-driven determination rather than innate impulse.

To do anything other than our described discipline would be mindful delusion, leaving us empty and unfulfilled. The dissatisfaction would be similar to catching a stocked rainbow trout on a spinner, rather than creeping down a river bank to land a wild brown trout rising to the Mayfly. The difference is marked, and any diversion from our self-imposed standards was not worth entertaining.

Our aesthetic is not for everyone, nor is it original. Other falconers will have their own variations on the theme and it is all absolutely subjective. To us, the two markers of excellence would be: (i) steady dogs, running to field-trial standards, who could be relied on to hold a point for lengthy periods, as well as not taking off into the blue yonder once the flush was executed, and (ii) high-mounting, disciplined, pure peregrine falcons of natural mindset, flying with a determined purpose, maintaining a rapid wing beat, loyal and expectant of a flush to stoop.

These markers are sought after and similarly developed by falconers on the western plains of America, hunting duck or the much larger sage grouse, for instance. They are also desired on the lowlands of Europe by falconers hunting partridge and pheasant. Invariably, hawking red grouse with a male peregrine (known as a tiercel, which is approximately one-third smaller than the female) in the Scottish Highlands, with all the mitigating hardships and distractions, *is,* without bias, the hardest discipline and aesthetic to achieve in falconry.

I'd argue that hawking red grouse in its purest form, as Stu described, is also one of the most dangerous, potently addictive variants of this compulsive artform. Stooping falcons from over a grand and catching red grouse in breathtaking style is hard to achieve; each attempt is often unsuccessful due to the tiniest of variables. The mindset that drives a falconer to step back onto the moor each time is akin to the most heavily afflicted gambling addict, betting on continual long odds, unable to shake their ambitions and self-belief in their methodology.

The red grouse is the pinnacle quarry for the peregrine falcon and pointing dog. Stu was one of the great exponents of the pointer. He and Mandy produce well-decorated, loving pointers that were a testament to his dedication, vision and continuation of the breed – a breed undoubtedly stronger for his input. The pointer was a breed I knew little of, until I met Stu

The Pointer

The English pointer has ascended to the summit of what our ancestors envisioned over 1,000 years ago. Now, some 11 centuries later, the pointer still remains at the top of its game, looking down upon his contemporaries that participate in the discipline of setting game.

✎©Amelia Siddle

The initial sculpting of the breed began in the Middle Ages, probably in Spain, and the dogs were aptly termed *Spainels* (not Spaniels). Their early prevalence corresponded with agricultural growth in Europe, when opening large expanses of countryside resulted in an increase in the partridge population. There was a clear need to separate blood- and boar-hounds from bird-dogs; however, we had to wait until the early 13th century for early breed descriptions to arise from German and Italian writers. They described dogs with falling ears that knew of both bird and beast, with powers derived from their sense of smell as well as training around birds. In 1387, it is suggested that longer-haired setting dogs (a derivative of the spaniel) arrived in France. This chien d'oisel or 'falcon-dog' is the first real incarnation of the English pointer's ancestor, and its description makes for fun reading:

'...these dogs have many good qualities, and bad ones also. A handsome falcon-dog should have a massive head, and large, well-made body, his coat being white or cinnamon colour (canele),

because these are the most beautiful and of this colour there are many excellent; they should not be too hairy, and the end of the tail should be tufted (espiee). The good qualities of these dogs are that they are very faithful to their masters, and follow them anywhere without being lost. They go also in front of birds willingly, ranging and making play with their tails, and find all birds and all beasts, but their proper business is at the partridge and the quail. For the man who has a good goshawk or falcon, lanner or tassel-hawk, and a good sparrow-hawk, they are very useful, and also when one teaches them to set their game they are good for taking partridges and quail with the net; they are also good, when broken to the river, for a bird that is diving. . . . And as one talks of a greyhound of Britain, the boarhounds and bird-dogs come from Spain.' (Des Deduiz de la Chasse, chapter xx.).

It is highly probable that this breed first came to England from France, and that these dogs' ancestors likely travelled through Spain in a relatively short space of time, some 50 years earlier. Remarkably, the majority of the founding stock may have arrived in a single delivery, when in 1624 a hugely valuable and thoughtful gift was made by the French King Louis XIII to arguably the most famous falconer in English History, James I (James VI of Scotland). Louis gifted 16 casts (i.e. 32 individuals) of hawks, along with horses and setting dogs, and even sent falconers to instruct on their use. If this story is apocryphal, then these falcon dogs would likely have been the imports of high-ranking army officers returning from Europe after the Peace of Utrecht in 1713.

Having been largely introduced in England by the mid-1700s for use in falconry, this 'falcon-dog' was now in the hands of English stockmanship. It was being used in other fieldsports, such as bird hunting with bows and arrows and primitive crossbows, and also setting and flushing partridges into long nets. However, the catalyst for the pointer's continued modification and the eventual establishment of the breed can be attributed to the advent of the gun and the soaring popularity of shooting. There was a requirement to refine the spainel/setting hound used for flushing game into nets and under falcons into a steadier dog that could cover the ground at a faster pace, provide a higher frequency of finds, and wait patiently on its finds before flushing on command, thus providing greater sport for the gun and falcon alike. In the hands of English stockmen, it took only 100 years of selective breeding to establish the English pointer that we recognise today. It's a breed that developed in true symmetry; a congruent growth of body, brain and game-finding ability.

©Amelia Siddle

Given that Stu and Manders bred such good pointers, this part of the equation was already taken care of. Moreover, I could pull favours with some of my old college chums and gain access to some very prestigious upland estates that held good numbers of grouse. This left us with the final predicament: acquiring the peregrines necessary to meet the challenge.

"We don't want none of them fuckin' puddled Frankenstein falcons," Stu announced with the strongest of resolve. He exhaled, and from behind the smokescreen I saw a pair of resolute and piercing eyes staring straight into mine. Stu clearly hated the imprinted and hybrid incarnates of the peregrine falcon made possible by selective breeding. In his mind, the peregrine was to be revered in her true form, unsullied by hybridisation or psychological manipulation. In his next breath he said, "We want to hunt with the wolf, not play with a labradoodle."

*****

The Peregrine

For the vast majority of falconry's history, the birds involved were taken directly from the wild, either as chicks (when they were known as 'eyasses'), first-years ('passagers') or adults ('haggards'). Britain was no exception, and a government-run application scheme was implemented in the twentieth century to manage the taking of birds for falconry. However, the 1960s saw a precipitous decline in peregrine populations as a result of environmental toxins, (especially DDT, which fatally thinned eggshells), and members of the British Falconers' Club elected to voluntarily halt wild-take applications. For a while, falconers had to make do with imported lanner, saker, and lugger falcons from Africa and Eurasia, and whilst some limited success was had, these desert falcons were poorly suited to the British weather. Meanwhile, those few peregrines already in captivity were put into speculative breeding pairs.

Progress was initially slow, proceeding by trial, error, and luck, but a small breeding pool was eventually established. In the USA, a more concerted effort by falconer-scientists at Cornell University in the 1980s led to a minor revolution, as artificial insemination (AI) – facilitated by the hand-rearing of young falcons – became routine. AI is now the dominant mode of falcon propagation, and incidentally offers the opportunity for hybridisation (which had occasionally occurred 'naturally' between captive peregrines and saker falcons). Peregrines are most commonly crossed with the larger species, such as the saker and the tundra-dwelling gyrfalcon but the possible combinations are myriad, and hybrids involving much smaller species such as the merlin, American kestrel, and aplomado falcon are not uncommon. Such is the closeness of the falcon gene pool, a large proportion of first-generation hybrids are fertile, so it is possible to cross again – by breeding, for example, a gyrfalcon-peregrine into a peregrine-saker falcon – and have a good old cocktail of genetics from which to select progeny characteristics.

Falcon propagation has gained sufficient traction to reach an industrial scale. Without doubt there is an opportunity for breeders to play God and shape falcons in ways that differ from the wild type, and it appears that we are already on that journey. We know falcon species are receptive to physical changes brought about by selective breeding, so there is no reason to think that falcons would somehow be resistant to behavioural changes, too.

*****

Stu found himself living through the fastest transition in falconry since its inception. Falconry in the UK was no longer a craft where the tools were exclusively authentic. The artform was developing an industrial, clinical footing, and the peregrine falcon that had fought hard for its existence on the cliff-face – the one he loved and revered – was beginning to acquire new identities.

Stu's eyes would tighten when notions of falconry less authentic than his were mentioned. Hybridising any falcon was an ethical boundary that Stu would never cross. In his mind, the peregrine should be kept pure. It was sacrilege to do anything other with its divinity. "A wild psyche is the peregrine's natural psyche," he'd say. Conversation would not be free from expletives at the very thought that, someday, due to the culmination of this new breeding industry and indiscriminate, reckless, cash-hungry breeders, a *Falco peregrinus domesticus* might be in the offing.

Taking a chick from the wild was not an option for us, that activity having been illegal since the 1960s. There was only one place Stu wanted to source our peregrines from, and that was his good friend, Andy Hollidge. Hollidge is a very accomplished long-time falconer and ex-gamekeeper. In Stu's mind, Hollidge possessed the most desirable peregrines in the country. Only once Hollidge's peregrines had met his criteria were they carefully selected and paired for breeding. He would only buy in, hunt and breed from those individual peregrines that showed behavioural and physical characteristics he deemed desirable. Hollidge still remains the authority on captive-bred lines – so much so that he is known fondly as *"The Knowledge"*. Not only do his falcons have to be large in form, broad set, thick legged with big feet, but importantly they need to have come from a proven pedigree of high-mounting, busy winged and aggressive-hunting ancestry.

Stu had great admiration for Hollidge's top breeding falcon, a fine peregrine that shared the same name as his beloved pointer, Jess. Hollidge's Jess was the latest progeny to be bred from a famed hunting tiercel called Touchwood. Touchwood would fly lowland quarry in the vast skies of Ashwell, in Hertfordshire. On crisp, frosty mornings, Touchwood would regularly eat up the high-pressure blue skies, ascending to a fast-flickering dot glistening in the sunlight. When Touchwood disappeared beyond the range of the naked eye, Hollidge would use his 10x50 binoculars to watch him pull overhead, then he'd send in his pointer bitch, Dixie (bred by Stu), for the flush. Excited recollections of such stoops earned Hollidge his other nickname, *Three-Grand-Andy*.

Touchwood was bred by staunch peregrine proponent, Ken McDougall. Going back further in Touchwood's ancestry, his mother, Blanche, came from two very capable and sought-after lines from falconer, breeder and author Ray Turner (author of *Gamehawk*). In a long flying career, Blanche took a variety of game, including woodcock, duck, pheasant, partridge and red grouse. She was paired with a fantastic tiercel known throughout the land as P.J., who proficiently hunted over 120 head of game, including grouse, before successfully breeding at the age of three. McDougall was aware of how lucky he was to be in possession of such a great family line of peregrines in Blanche, and not simply because she excelled. He recalled that, on one occasion, Blanche absconded for a few days as a juvenile. After a week at large, a quick-thinking local gamekeeper spotted her on a telegraph pole. He cobbled together a lure from a dried-up dead swallow he found and a piece of string that was being used to hold the mudguard of his bike in place. He threw the makeshift lure on the ground, and thankfully Blanche took the bait. The keeper threw his Barbour jacket over her; however, Blanche outwitted him and scuttled down the sleeve to escape again. In spite of this ordeal, her hunger was sufficient to make her gullible enough to be fooled twice, and the whole cycle was repeated, save for the wax jacket holding her firm. Finally, she was back on the block.

It was late summer in 2010, and we were very much counting our peregrines before they hatched. Nevertheless, Stu secured our names at the top of Hollidge's list for this sought-after and hotly anticipated clutch. If there was any truth to the argument that behavioural characteristics can pass from parent to chick, then Hollidge's chicks would be stooping out of their eggshells! The following year had all the makings of an exciting season. All we could do was bide our time, ride out the autumn and winter, and hope for breeding success next spring.

Dobson

A 250-acre field of wheat, drainage ditch, crap hedge, shelter belt or spruce plantation followed by another 250 acres of wheat, drainage ditch, crap hedge or spruce plantation. The landscape of East Anglia soon became as flat, boring, predictable, uninteresting and as tediously drawn out as the local dialect. Make no mistake, the villages and hamlets are few and nicely spread in comparison to the outskirts of London, just 50 miles south, but this region is farmed so intensively that to the knowing eye it now forms a depressing industrial landscape. The granting of a new solar farm and wind turbine installation on Six Mile Bottom, although necessary, proved too much of an encroachment that would deaden my soul. Having had a taste of the wilds of Scotland, I found it beyond comparison, and missed the rivers, mountains, forests and wildlife.

As sometimes happens in life, a phone call out of the blue provided the perfect solution. It was my good friend Andrew Dobson. "Woz," – as I was sometimes known – "I've just taken a job as a research associate for the University of Stirling. You're up for a move back to Scotland, yes? Need a housemate? Well, if you find a cottage in the country, you've got one. I'll be ready to move in a few weeks."

Dobson hails from a largely Scottish family. He's a former falconer and Oxford alumnus who grew up – much to his irritation – in the southeast of England. He grew up flying falcons in the vast open skies of Warboys, Cambridgeshire, and learned his craft over a few extended summers under the mentorship of Leonard and Diana Durman-Walters in the Scottish Borders. It was under Len's tutelage that he began to make falconry hoods, doing so professionally to keep his university bar tab in check. Although we were at very different universities, it was through falconry that I had befriended Dobson some years earlier. We worked together for a small falconry outfit in Edinburgh. Throughout the summer holidays we'd tour Historic Scotland sites, providing flying demonstrations in the grounds of various forts and castles.

Me at Fort George ~ 2000 📷©Dave Warren

I was extremely jealous of Dobson's ability to train hawks and also make hoods. His proposition would put me one step closer to realising my new falconry ambitions. I had a few months to wait before our peregrines hatched, and so I seized on the opportunity, replying: "Teach me how to make hoods and I'll get us a place, sure." Dobson, as usual, had a joyful response. "Sounds agreeable, although I must warn you, it's a shit hobby."

The move back over the border felt right and, with a huge debt of gratitude to Richard Clarke, I handed in my notice and left Six Mile Bottom. I soon found a two-bed, wooden shepherd's cottage beneath the north-facing Burnfoot ridgeline, about a mile or so from Gargunnock. It was called Knock O'Ronald Cottage, which we inevitably changed to Ronald's Knocking Box, then (for ease), simply "The Box". There was an overgrown garden to the rear of The Box left in gay abandon. The garden was big enough to build some accommodation (known as a mews) for my expectant peregrine, and a much-needed woodshed. Mike was only half an hour up the road and was easily bribed to help us with the build. It was great to settle back in Scotland with my close friends for company. Things had really fallen into place.

True to his word, Dobson equipped me with hood patterns, leather, tools and hood blocks. His mentoring never went beyond placing an open copy of the 2005 edition of *The Falconer* containing an article he'd penned and illustrated, titled *Making The Dutch Hood*. Dobson was blunt and unvarying in his teaching style. Each time I struggled and asked for help, he would say, "Turn to page 63, re-read the article, follow it and don't fuck it up." And yet, each time I would stubbornly ignore his advice, leave the journal on the shelf and remain resolute. I was convinced that my pig-headedness and the slowly-refining skill being developed in my fingers and thumbs would eventually turn out a good hood.

I found hood-making seriously addictive. The incremental measures of improvement are tiny, yet the magnitude of each refinement was so great it fuelled the desire to go again, to do better. Before I knew it, I was discarding my most recent effort in favour of cutting a new pattern from the leather, wanting to make a better one. In hood-making, it is impossible to correct imperfections – they remain part of the hood for life. Uneven, loose or torn stitching, or asymmetrical blocking, will remain a permanent feature of your latest effort. When terminal mistakes happen, such as a skewed beak opening or ripped brace slits, you need to accept that you've spent two days making *another* dog chew.

The fundamental lesson a hoodmaker needs to learn is that the most important piece of tooling on the hood is the bit you cut out and throw away – the beak opening. Without a proper beak opening, the hood will not fit the falcon. The fit needs to ensure that the cere is exposed, in order to prevent bruising and sores. The lower jaw or gape must be wide and exposed, to enable regurgitation and the passing of casting materials.

Any hoodmaker will empathise with experiences not too dissimilar to those described by Philip Glasier – in his book *As the Falcon Her Bells* – when he made his first half-decent hood for his falcon, Greensleeves. Discovering it fitted, he added the finishing touches and numbered it 42, writing that the other 41 had been duds. I easily made 50 attempts, probably more, before stitching a decent hood that was skived to suit a tiercel peregrine. I think the desire of the hoodmaker goes far beyond the practical purpose. It fuels an excellence in creativity and craftsmanship. Some of the world's top hoodmakers aren't even falconers. For me, the ultimate goal in hood-making was to create both an elegant and beautifully fitting hood that gave me a sense of pride and made my stride that bit longer when I walked out onto the moor.

However, for all the notoriety and wonderfully snobbish grandeur I attached to having a posh hood for the moor, it has to be remembered that all hoods used on falcons are fundamentally a welfare tool. And, like any tool, they can be correctly used, incorrectly used, used unnecessarily, poorly treated and, indeed, may not even be the right tool for the job.

Stitching a hood for Ballyhoo. 📷©Dave Warren

The clocks fell back and winter consumed The Box. I used the dark evenings to master the art of hood-making, in particular the traditional Dutch pattern as described in Dobson's article. After many, many attempts enduring turmoil and frustration, I began to turn out some worthy efforts that were fit for purpose, adding fuel to my infatuation with this cottage industry. The fancy hoods took pride of place in the living room. Each day I looked at them, the anticipation grew. I was getting excited to roll them on my new peregrine. I just had to wait patiently for springtime.

By this time, Dobson had given up practising falconry, but like most falconers, retained the obsessive personality. At Oxford, he'd transferred his attention to athletics, and now spent most evenings at the university running track at Stirling. On returning to The Box, Dobson would often peer-review academic papers written by his students. His scornful sighs amused me no end. I didn't need to look up from my stitchwork to know these exasperations were often a prequel to a "No," which would be followed by the busy scratching of his red biro. All in the service of making the next generation of budding scientists that bit sharper.

The thought of bringing a television into The Box repulsed both Dobson and me in equal measure. Neither of us missed staring at a screen, being drip-fed ghastly consumer dross. Instead, we'd busy ourselves hunting rabbit and pigeon to eat, then cooking, reading and battling with the fire, persuading unseasoned timber to burn. On occasion we'd venture to the pub or visit the local auction mart and purchase the various pieces of furniture, decor and kit we were missing; firstly some garden tools, then more elaborate items such as Queen Anne Chesterfield wing-back sitting chairs, a roll-top bureau for hood-making, vintage bookshelves, fire irons, a brass telescope – that sort of thing. To the suburbanite, the absence of a television raises the question: *what on earth do you put the furniture around?* To us, such a predicament was insignificant and quickly overcome as the living room became a lot more interesting than a 32-inch flatscreen. The auction house provided no end of intricacies that decorated the cottage; a 1939 hand-cranked Singer sewing machine was one of my favourite purchases. I used it for sewing braces for hoods and repairing clothes. Dobson bought himself a 1920s Underwood typewriter and produced essential communications for his own amusement. These quips were typed 'neath the glow of his oil-fired lamp. Next to his lamp was his brass telescope, which was put to good use spotting wild peregrines and ravens on the crags of the Burnfoot Hills.

The Box quickly began to resemble Uncle Monty's cottage from *Withnail and I*. We knew we had the look and feel about right when I invited a girl I was rather keen on back to The Box. After I'd poured her a cup of loose-leaf tea from the antique tea service, she looked confusedly about the room at the taxidermy, hanging tapestries, antique bookcases, basket-hilted swords, drinks globe and deer antlers until, in total bewilderment, she broke her silence: "Do you two rent this place from a weird elderly couple?"

The assembly of antiquities in The Box might have outwardly appeared frivolous, however most items were bought for pence at the auction house. The place was threadbare when we moved in. We had few possessions and nothing to make the cottage homely. As we added such oddities, The Box developed a character conducive to our interests and lifestyles, a dwelling in the very real sense of the word. We loved spending time in an environment that guarded against unwanted media flooding and allowed us to continue our crafts – hood-making in my case, and academia in Dobson's. Ralph Brown would stretch out in front of the fire and only stir when we'd reach over him for firewood. Being somewhat withdrawn from modern intrusions and living a fairly wild existence gave rise to a self-sufficiency campaign and rejection of the supermarket. The only thing that wasn't ideal was the overgrown grass outside, as we were without a lawnmower. We knew perfectly well that our mode of living was unavailable to most of the population, and that we were therefore lucky rather than righteous. Nonetheless, we felt unavoidably smug about the extent to which our needs were met by the fields and woods rather than the town and its shops. Our meals were seasoned with satisfaction and appreciation; the pigeon, rabbit and pheasant were richer, and the blackcurrant jam so much sweeter.

We were not typical tenants of the property and, after a period of time living in The Box, we struck up good relations with our neighbour, himself a tenant on the estate who farmed the hillfoots with a small herd of sheep. On one occasion, I met him walking off the hill as I was carrying a couple of freshly shot pigeons in my hand. He was fetching two old draft ewes back to the farm to provide them with much-needed supplementary feed. We talked about how he was reduced to barely a subsistence farmer, struggling with the challenges of his industry and environment – he joked there was better and tastier meat on my pigeons than on the rather sorry-looking sheep stumbling ahead of us, capable of commanding just £20 at the sales. Thinking of a way to help him, I offered up a suggestion. "You can put them in our garden if you like, there's good grass and we need a lawnmower – I'll swap them for these pigeons." The farmer laughed and agreed to the exchange. I walked back to The Box to tell Dobson the good news. "Sorted the lawnmower situation. Thank me later."

So the sheep stayed in the garden for a month or two and, in exchange for a bucket of fresh water, kept our grass in order until the grazing was reduced to slim pickings, whereupon we offered them back to the farmer. However, he wasn't so sure they'd hold condition on the hill, nor if they were worth selling. Clearly in two minds, he said, "I think you boys should take care of them."

So we did. I was transported back to my 12-year-old youth and taught Dobson all I knew of butchery. Between us we skinned and jointed the unfortunate beasts in the woodshed, filling our freezer with a volume of meat that would have cost us handsomely had we bought it from the supermarket. We cooked the mutton as slowly as it took our hands to stop smelling of sheep. It was quite delicious. The farmer must have liked the pigeons we dropped on his doorstep, for after a week or two we discovered the garden gate was once again tied with bailer twine, the bucket of water topped up, and a new 'lawnmower' resided in our garden. This tidy arrangement was repeated five or six times over the next couple of years.

*****

Ballyhoo

Hollidge had a fortuitous breeding season, and our peregrines were *finally* ready to collect. Both falcons were eight and a half weeks old, having hatched just three days apart. At that age, they were big healthy fledglings, able to move around the aviary and feed themselves, and they were just about fully feathered. Their legs and torso were strong enough to withstand being on tether, and as such, they were ready to start discovering life beyond the aviary. I left Dobson in charge of Ralph Brown and headed south to collect our new housemate.

I arrived at Stu's on Friday so we were ready to make the short journey to Hollidge's home the following morning. The evening was once again spent in his warm, homely kitchen, filled with nostalgic stories and predictions of splendour from both hawk and hound. I loved catching up with Stu and Mands. Nothing much had changed, and before long they both had me roaring with laughter. A little later in the evening I opened the shackles of my toolbox, took out a fine roll of Kangaroo leather, and moving all the old coffee cups and pouches of tobacco off the kitchen table, cleared a space to cut fresh anklets and jesses to fit onto our peregrines. The leather was treated using a leather balm, left to soak in overnight. This treatment would eliminate the possibility of sores occurring once the anklets were affixed to the falcons. Stu, happy with my leatherwork and the fact his hands remained free from leather grease, instructed me to make his hawk's anklets as he rolled another cigarette. Feeling a little embarrassed but encouraged that he liked my leatherwork, I then pulled a hood I had made for him out of the toolbox. It was one of my best efforts to date, with a grouse-feather plume on the top. Stu knew it was simply too good for the occasion and explained it would be a waste to use it on a new young falcon. It was more decorative than working, but nevertheless he was delighted. Stu had a well-used Pineo hood that he wanted to use for his falcon. He took the Pineo hood down from the wall and replaced it with the one I'd just gifted to him and said reassuringly, "Don't worry, it'll come off the hook when the time is right."

We arrived at Hollidges's home by mid-morning, beyond excited to pick up the sibling peregrines. It is always best to transport young falcons without food in their crops to prevent travel sickness. As such, Hollidge hadn't put food in the aviary for 24 hours prior to our arrival. Human provisions were, however, laid out in abundance for our arrival. Stu was not shy about ripping into the tea cakes that Hollidge's daughter, Maisy, had lovingly baked for elevenses.

As the three of us chatted about the falcons, we became increasingly intrigued, until we could wait no longer. All of us were keen to get the measure of our new hunting partners, so we headed for Hollidge's garage. The relaxing tea and delicious sugary cakes helped steady the nerves. Stu had a cigarette and watched me lay out the leather jess, anklets and equipment on the workbench. We handed Hollidge the hoods – my effort and Stu's choice Pineo – then stood waiting for Hollidge to reappear. The door opened and Hollidge was cradling a falcon wearing my hood – it had to be mine! The falcon was wrapped safely in a tea towel, which cloaked all of his features. All emotions had to remain in check; it was an absolute requirement to be very business-like and efficient in attaching the anklets to the falcons. This was something I'd done hundreds of times before. It was a simple, slick operation where speed was of the essence to reduce stress and trauma. It was quite a rude awakening for our peregrines. Having been brought up in seclusion and kept secret from the outside world, they were now taken from their aviary and subjected to handling and manipulation. If the falcons could see, the experience would be so much worse. It filled me with much pride to see that my hood fitted him well. Professionalism was key and there was no room for gushing thoughts and emotions, so I quelled the desire to look too much at the feathers, the feet, the beak, to imagine him tearing up the skies. No – the attaching of equipment demanded unwavering concentration and speed of hand.

We repeated the operation for Stu's falcon, and before long we were standing outside. Now was the time to marvel at two immaculate, feather-perfect falcons. Hollidge had produced some exemplary peregrines. Both falcons were behaving as one would expect: a bite of the anklets here, a scratch of the hood there, but they were mostly in a withdrawn state. About two cigarettes, a cup of tea and a fairy cake later, we began to see the peregrines relax. Small clouds of dust erupted from the falcons each time they shook and roused. To the untrained eye, rousing looks quite violent, as if the bird is having a two-second seizure, but they are simply adjusting. In unison the two falcons began to preen, realign their feathers and use their beaks to have a good feel of the unfamiliar equipment attached to their legs.

Before the birds had a chance to become overly animated and jump about their tether, Hollidge began to unwind the garden hose. One trick to avoid the catastrophe of snapping a feather is to gently wet the flight feathers until they are soaked. The falcon's innate response to getting wet is to stand still and dry off, thus wetting the feathers will literally dampen high spirits. Wet feathers make the wings heavy, so the falcon is less likely to damage vulnerable flight feathers because she is less inclined to flail her wings. Should a feather snap, it will not be naturally replaced until the following spring, owing to the falcon's natural moulting cycle, leaving the peregrine disfigured for a full year. It is important not to soak her to the skin as this will shock her – it's a gentle wetting of the feathers, not a waterboarding.

With an 8-hour journey back to Scotland ahead of me, I was keen to get on the road. Hollidge used the gentle spray setting and we began to wet the tail and flight feathers of my tiercel. This was the first time I got to hold him properly on the fist. The hood fitted him well and caused him precious little irritation. He felt heavy, stocky, and his big toes curled around my fingers as he gripped my glove – he was a stonker! Whilst spraying him down I had a word to myself, consciously reiterating just how precious this falcon and this opportunity were. I knew that realising my ambition to fly him at red grouse would require dedication and the harnessing of all my skill. A quote from *Good Will Hunting* jumped into my head: *"Now no more shenanigans. No more tomfoolery. No more ballyhoo."* Ballyhoo, I pondered and smiled. That's quirky; let's see if it sticks.

Having settled my peregrine safely on his cadge, it was time to pay Hollidge. In 1936, Falconer and author Gilbert Blain wrote peregrine chicks from the nest were said to be worth from thirty shillings up to two pounds. Fast forward a little to the 1960s, when M.H. Woodford writes that the bird is worth thirty pounds plus tips. Half a century later and I paid Andy three hundred and fifty pounds for mine, a very agreeable and fair price. Hollidge and he had no reason to discount his sought-after peregrines, nor absorb any of the rearing and registration cost on my behalf. His agreement with Stu, however, was slightly different.

Stu's staunch viewpoint was to always take the money out of hawk and hound within a close syndicate of friends. This would ensure that no matter what their predicament, those within the circle always had a decent hawk or pointer available to satisfy their rage to practise falconry. Most falconers fly 'neath the cruellest of clouds' and there is an all-too-common trend that great hunting falcons do not endure a decade of successive hunting – they are susceptible to injury or die before their time. Electrocution, predation and loss is a more likely demise for hunting falcons than disease or illness in the aviary. Wrapped in cotton wool and staying within the safety of the aviary however, the life expectancy of a peregrine is pushed to the high teens, sometimes beyond.

By taking money out of the equation, it would ensure the syndicate works together and enjoys seeing the prodigies develop. By being adventurous and flying the falcons with plenty of liberty, the group would get a chance to thoroughly evaluate and only breed from those hawks or hounds with the best attributes – making us responsible custodians of the heritage. In line with this viewpoint, Hollidge and Stewart agreed a straight swap – one of Stu's pointer pup bitches for one of Hollidges's falcons.

I travelled back to Scotland and made it to The Box in good time. Dobson was impressed and remarked on the impressive size and condition of my new tiercel and, surprisingly, he wasn't rude or full of scorn at the name Ballyhoo. I placed the falcon on his indoor perch. There was little more to do with him that night other than rest him and let Ralph Brown have a sniff. I poured myself a glass of wine, marvelled at Ballyhood and gave Stu a quick call to let him know we had arrived without incident and the name Ballyhoo had stuck.

"I've called mine Gilbert," Stu announced. I thought Gilbert was a strange name for a female peregrine, but perhaps it had some significance. Maybe it was the name of a relative or previous hawk he had flown. I was wrong. Gilbert was quite broad, and when she fluffed up and sat contented on his lawn, in Stu's eyes her shape looked a bit like a rugby ball. As he placed her in his mews that afternoon, he looked up and there was a Gilbert rugby ball – it was as simple as that. Stu must have had countless opportunities to name hawks and falcons. His days of choosing tiresome cliches such as Icarus, Slasher, Gripper or Lightning were long buried. To him, the name Gilbert was amusing. From opposite ends of the country, we set about taming our sibling peregrines, Ballyhoo and Gilbert, who in our eyes, were undoubtedly the best peregrines available.

It was day three of desensitising Ballyhoo. Up until now he had mostly kept himself composed on the glove, yet still refused to touch any of the food on offer to him. Together we'd binge listen to several radio broadcasts, namely the full *Dad's Army* radio archives and many episodes of *The News Quiz* and *I'm Sorry I Haven't a Clue*. Dobson and Ralph Brown had once made Ballyhoo weary, but they were now subjects of inquisition. From the moment the hood was rolled off I could tell this manning (taming) session was going to be different. Ballyhoo's giant inky-black eyes were unmasked. He quickly familiarised himself with his unchanged surroundings, then half-cocked his head to one side to focus on the food I held in the glove. Standing firm for a few minutes, Ballyhoo then dared to reach for the food. He craned downwards, his beak gripping the quail leg held tightly between my gloved fingers and, on feeling some resistance, he aborted his intention and stood tall once more. He was wide-eyed and ready to take flight, so I remained motionless, averted my gaze and froze. After several very long seconds, his next movement was to once again tilt his head, nod, then gauge focus on the morsel of meat on offer (vetching). Half-bent, he quickly grabbed some of the quail feathers that dressed the outstretched quail leg. He ripped at them and shook his head, sending the feathers wide before standing tall, once more wide-eyed, motionless, withdrawn and expectant of peril. There was no reaction to his undertakings, nor change to his environment, so he took aim and again plucked at the feathers. It was at this point I knew I had him. Finding that no harm came from his daring, Ballyhoo felt safe in his convictions and continued to pluck in earnest – the quail feathers beginning to fall around my feet. Relaxing further, he adjusted his footing to get a better purchase on the quail leg and continued to prepare his meal. He was intent on feeding rather than flying away. I remained motionless, suspended in the sort of locked-in state I knew was necessary to accomplish a good first session with Ballyhoo. The slightest tension in my arm, movement in my fingers or wry smile might have been sufficient to unsettle him, and make him abort feeding.

It was a familiar feeling that brewed. I had gotten many falcons to readily feed on the fist, but when each falcon does so for the first time, it evokes the same feelings of excitement and pride. It's the indication that you've gained an element of acceptance, and that the falcon is content to enter into a working relationship. Food is the primary reinforcing tool available to the falconer. Falcons care little for excited voice tones and tickles under the chin as a reward. Ballyhoo had an appetite and was feeding, and I now had a means of reinforcing behaviour and encouraging further development.

Ballyhoo discarded the unwanted quail leg bone, throwing it to the floor with his beak. He then ran his beak over his talons demonstrating that he was satisfied. Falcons naturally clean and sharpen their beaks (something known as frecking), after they've finished a meal, as it prevents the beak from overgrowing. This was my cue. I held his hood in my right hand and gradually raised it towards his feet; this is the crucial time to maintain a progressive continuous movement and roll the hood on. Any hesitation in the hood's application would likely result in the falcon taking objection and bating. Ballyhoo remained still, and the hood rolled perfectly into place. Striking the hood braces marked the end of a successful session and I sighed with ecstatic relief. Once in the hood, Ballyhoo had a rouse and even began to have a quick preen of himself, demonstrating contentment. I returned him to the mews for the night, feeling relieved. The entire session was positive, and I could build on this progress. This made me excited for the next day; I just needed to remain patient.

From the point that Ballyhoo first fed on the fist, my mission thereafter was never to have him bate. Although this was extremely unlikely, it was a very worthy ambition. Like all the falcons I had tamed in the past, I knew it would probably take a few days to cement feeding on the fist and for him to become fully relaxed in the home. Ballyhoo had a good reserve of 'puppy fat' that lessened the need for rigorous feeding whilst he acclimatised to his new environment. I knew this process was so important to get right. Progression to the next phase couldn't be achieved until I had banked up sufficient trust and he was settled into a familiar routine.

Ralph Brown snoozing, Ballyhoo inquisitive. ©Dave Warren

Slowly, Ballyhoo began to accept the goings-on of the cottage and turned a blind eye to Ralph Brown stretching in his bed or Dobson ruffling papers and pouring leaf tea. It was time to offer him a little bit more exposure, so I began to take him outside to feed him. The garden bench was positioned facing into the breeze and we sat with our backs to the cottage. Striking the hood braces, I rolled the hood off his head and exposed Ballyhoo to the outside world. Wide-eyed, he gazed into the Burnfoot crags and to the horizon. He was flooded with stimuli – Lord knows what he made of it. I snapped him out of his trance by wiggling my fingers, animating the pheasant leg on which he stood. The sensation of movement under his toes was sufficient to trigger his impulse to feed – akin to prey twitching in its last throes of life – and Ballyhoo craned over and began to pull at it. Feeding was not as carefree and rigorous as it was inside the cottage – distraction restricted his inhibitions to feed with vigour. There were prolonged periods spent gazing, detecting movement or abhorrent shapes, such as raven's moving from crag to crag, that would sway his attention. Nevertheless, Ballyhoo remained composed. He fed a little, roused, fed some more, then threw the leg bone to the floor. As normal, I presented the hood and brought him back inside. We sat and fed outside for the next three evenings, getting used to the great outdoors and imagining what was beyond the horizon.

In order to let Ballyhoo range freely to the horizon, I needed a means to recall him. This would be achieved by simply training him to zoom back to a lure garnished with food as soon as it was pulled from my hawking bag. The lure represents a dead prey item. It's a faux carcass from which the falcon will want to feed. Often it is a small leather pad about the size of your fist, but it can be anything so long as the falcon accepts it and recognises it as food. I lashed together some pheasant wings. This wing lure is lightweight, animates well when dangled and triggers the falcon's impulse to commit, increasing its efficiency.

I needed to ensure Ballyhoo wouldn't be unnerved at the presentation of the lure and make sure he associated it with great reward. The very first introduction needed to be very calm and unceremonious to prevent Ballyhoo having an adverse reaction to its unveiling. All Ballyhoo was familiar and content with was quietly hopping to the glove for a repeat reward. Rummaging in the vest and removing a big foreign object, like a lure, could cause him to frighten. The success of this new introduction would be marked by his calm measure, capturing and reinforcing the new behaviour of feeding from the lure. The distance at which Ballyhoo would travel to the lure was insignificant, nor the time taken to brave the action. Ballyhoo just needed to be confident and assured of his actions.

When training any animal, it is most useful to emit a noise to mark the exact moment a desired behaviour is met. The noise can be simply verbalising *yes* or *good*, it could be the *click* of a clicker or a *peep* of a whistle. It matters little, so long as the noise is heard and understood by the animal and is a consistent marker of having achieved the criteria. The noise is known as a bridge, as it bridges the gap between completing what is being asked for, and receiving the reward for doing so. The use of a bridge massively accelerates training by removing confusion, capturing inadvertent behaviour and cementing repetition. Falcons, I believe, have no ambition to *please* us. They do, however, remember what they did in order to get food, and often repeat that behaviour; bridging speeds up their learning.

Prior to the recall, if the falcon's actions are bridged and reinforced, the falcon will be filled with confidence. She will be more likely to come in, hard, and take the lure without hesitation. The next day she will likely fly in a similar manner but, more importantly, expect reward at the sound of the bridge, even when it is not visible. This makes the bridge a good precursor to a stoop, and can be used to bring the falcon into position and focus. That said, if you don't know how to bridge correctly, you will confuse the falcon and regress training.

Using a bridge to train behaviour is something I'd always done whilst training falcons at the Safari Park. I knew the method worked well and decided to use it with Ballyhoo. I just needed a whistle. I remembered to my childhood, and reached into the box that contained my grandfather's wartime effects. His Acme Thunderer whistle produced a mighty blast that could be heard across a vast landscape. Who knows, I thought, maybe the sentimental attachment might just bring me some luck.

As was normal around feeding time, I went into the garden and collected Ballyhoo. I knelt next to his perch and he jumped onto the fist for a small reward and accepted the hood. I walked into the cottage and could tell he was expectant and keen to feed. I attached a longer training line, known as a creance, to his swivel in order to slightly extend his range beyond his normal leash length. Noticing the creance line, Dobson took the opportunity to look up and offer some advice for the occasion: "You're going for it then? Well, don't fuck it up."

Buoyed by his encouragement, I carried Ballyhoo away from the garden to the adjacent field. I knelt down, then wound out three feet of line and secured the creance handle to my hawking vest. I put the lure a few feet in front of me on the ground. It was garnished with half a quail breast and facing upwards. I struck the hood braces and rolled the hood from Ballyhoo's head. He stood wide-eyed at finding himself in a new predicament. I gently tweaked the lure line, causing the lure to become animated and grip his attention. Ballyhoo's response was to nod and try to ascertain what lay in front of him. In doing so, he half opened his wings – was this going to be a flight or fright moment, I wondered?

I moved my arm and held Ballyhoo a little closer to the lure. He remained on the fist, nodding, and leaned towards the quail, unsure whether to commit. With another quick tweak of the lure line to trigger his instincts, Ballyhoo braved a hop and landed next to the lure, then stuck out his leg and footed the quail tied to the twitching wings. I gave a very quick and quiet peep on the whistle as he snatched the lure.

Now feeling at his most vulnerable, and full of adrenaline, I knew it was paramount to stay still and not startle him. Ballyhoo quickly learned it was impossible to carry his prize away, and his instincts reverted to the next best option – to eat it as quickly as possible. He made short work of quaffing the soft quail breast and was looking unsure about what to do next. I lowered my glove with food held tightly in it. This was a familiar option, so he stepped up and ate his reward as I simultaneously hid the spent lure in my pocket. He remained steady throughout, and hooded – without objection. I took the decision to repeat the session. Usually, it is best at this point to quit whilst you're ahead, but only having eaten half of his prescribed ration and seemingly very focused, I had confidence there was more to be gained. I could reinforce that this lure was desirable and a safe place from which to feed. I tied half a quail breast to the lure and placed it about three feet away from me, before rolling Ballyhoo's hood from his head. He craned down and quickly responded to the twitching lure. This time he flew straight at it and grabbed the quail – a perfect introduction.

A couple of days passed, and each day I repeated dropping Ballyhoo to the lure to the point where it became unnecessary to repeat this exercise. He had a good comprehension of the lure, was bridged with a whistle every time, had been exposed whilst feeding and was indifferent to being picked up off the lure. It was now time to move to the next step in his training, recalling him at distance to a hung lure.

Stu was a great calming influence. Each evening we'd discuss the day's session. Stu always questioned how my falcon was reacting so he could draw on his wealth of experience to help me make rapid progress and prevent me regressing or making mistakes. Although he was 400 miles away, he somehow knew how to steer progress just by asking the right questions and listening to my descriptions. Stu spoke in encouraging tones and gave me faith in what I was doing. Dobson had been helping me recall Ballyhoo from one side of the field and we were now at the point where the creance was becoming a hindrance. Trusting Stu's words and my instincts, we decided it was time to remove the training line and let Ballyhoo fly free.

The session, in Ballyhoo's eyes, was to be consistent with the previous few days. There would be nothing new entering into the mix that might confuse or distract him. The only thing I'd do differently would be attaching a tracking device instead of the creance. The tracker is a very lightweight cell that emits an Ultra High Frequency (UHF) radio signal. Using a special antenna on the handheld receiver, you can aim the aerial and point it in the direction of the strongest signal, allowing you to walk in a straight line to find the falcon. Dobson obliged in his slipping duties, and twice Ballyhoo flew the length of the field, straight to the garnished lure that I dangled to the side of me. As was routine, I bridged him with a short blast of the whistle when he was close to taking the lure. That was it. Fairly unceremonious, even routine – except that Ballyhoo was now without tether, the creance line was redundant and Ballyhoo was free to go wherever he chose.

*****

Priming The Peregrine

Gilbert and Ballyhoo were now flying free and eagerly targeting the lure without issue. Stu's next phase was to condition the falcons in order to encourage and shape their behaviour to suit our hunting style. Stu insisted that we get the falcons fit and able to fly without their wings skipping a beat, flat out for about five minutes, in both calm and blustery conditions. With each wingbeat they'd create lift and race upwards, flying up on their tails as they powered to the cloud base.

"If I can tell the falcon is flying shit, then so will the grouse," Stu said as he explained that the red grouse is an astounding escapologist who needs no second invitation to clear the moor to evade a falcon. If the falcon is flying lazily on fixed wings it will not be taken seriously by the grouse – and rather than hiding from the falcon, the grouse will instead find the opportune moment to get on the wing and put untenable distance between themselves and their predator. However, if the falcon is flying in a commanding style, with aggressive, menacing vigour, eating up the sky, wings-a-blur and purposely gaining height locally, then the grouse will naturally remain clamped and hidden, there to be flushed at the perfect moment.

I had romanticised and indulged in the fantasy of hawking red grouse. Everything sounded very splendid around the kitchen table. In reality, however, the discipline of flying a gamehawk at such a wily quarry was fast becoming very daunting and taxing. To put Ballyhoo within touching distance of a red grouse, I needed to develop a punchy flying style, and the only way of achieving this was to correctly interpret Ballyhoo's efforts and intentions. It was up to me to correctly reward him and ready him for the following day's session. But where did I start?

"We'll kite 'em," Stu decided. "I can teach you all you need to know."

*****

The principles of kite training are quite simple. Instead of recalling the falcon to a hand-held lure, one attaches the lure to the kite string and uses the kite to raise the lure, putting the falcon's target, reward and stimulus at an altitude to suit progressive training. The theory behind the method is to condition the hawk to fly in a busy fashion, until you can guarantee ability for a set period of time – much like a track athlete would train for running 400, 800 or 1200 metres. Luckily for me, Dobson came equipped to The Box with his bespoke Dan Leigh kite. He was well versed in rigging the lure and launching the kite from his days flying his lanner falcon.

Dobson getting the kite airborne.

Me and Ballyhoo targeting the kite.

📷©Dave Warren

The presence of a kite is both daunting and threatening for the falcon. There is a natural aversion to flying 'neath the three-foot triangular sail, understandably similar to the Darwinian predisposition the falcon has to avoid flying below a Golden eagle. Therefore, just like introducing the lure, there must be an element of desensitising the falcon to the kite and a period where it must first learn its insignificance, then its attraction.

I had left the kite open and tied at all three corners to the garden fence of The Box. Ballyhoo had several days to attempt to fathom its obscure yet insignificant presence as he weathered on the lawn. Ballyhoo was fed close to the kite and was unmoved by its rattling on the fence. The plan was quite simple: we'd put the kite a couple of hundred feet in the air to make it less imposing, then hang the lure at about 50 feet from the ground. I'd stand under the lure and Dobson would release Ballyhoo from his usual spot at the far end of the field.

Ballyhoo took the lure suspended from the kite on the very first time of asking. He cocked his head to one side and looked at the kite, then he clocked the garnished lure pad dangling and animated on the kite rig above my head. After a quick nod of the head to get the measure of it, he bravely went straight for the lure. When he was a few metres from the lure, I bridged the behaviour using my grandfather's trench whistle. Ballyhoo was unwavering in his flight to the lure. He grasped the pad and held it tightly in his talons as the rig slid down the kite line, until it ended up on the floor. There he fed from the lure and paid little attention to the kite, after which I stepped him up as usual and re-hooded him. It was all very unceremonious, and he was oblivious to the significance of the progress he had made in his training. We repeated the exercise a few moments later, again without issue. This was a huge advancement, as it would soon enable me to get Ballyhoo eating up the skies. Until this point, he had only ever flown towards me from the far side of the field, having been released by Dobson. From this moment forth, I would be able to release him, and he would fly away from me to target the lure suspended under the kite.

Setting the kite at a few hundred feet the next day, I suspended the lure slightly higher on the kite line, at about 200 feet or so. Ballyhoo would not be able to fly to it in a straight line. Instead, he'd have to range a little further, go a little higher, arc round and return to the lure. I was asking him to show a higher degree of determination and push a little harder. This would be the farthest and highest he'd flown and there was a real danger he might get distracted and fly away. I stood in the field holding Ballyhoo, struck the hood braces and rolled the hood from his head. He looked at me, checked the horizon, and in doing so raised his head and caught a glimpse of the kite, and beneath it the lure. It must have surprised him to see it so far up in the air. Regardless, as soon as looked at it, he was off to secure it. I could see his head remained half-cocked as he flew. He didn't avert his gaze from the pad as he flew out 200 yards or so, arced round to level with the lure, then returned and grasped it. Once more he brought the rig down the kite line and found himself on the ground and feeding off the lure. This time I gave him the whole ration and didn't ask him to go again. He had clearly grasped the concept.

Over the next few weeks, I pushed the kite higher and demanded more from Ballyhoo. I asked him for one good workout a day to push his fitness, and I learned how to develop his style. Key indicators allowed me to assess his overall progress. I relayed my observations back to Stu on our daily phone call and he was able to offer suggestions to optimise performance.

With each session, Ballyhoo would range further and further, and climb higher and higher. From the lure suspended at 50 feet at the first time of asking, to half a grand within a week, and then beyond. He was doing well. I grew in confidence as he developed a busy snake-like pattern across the skies to reach the lure. I watched him face into the wind, and with each clip of his wing gain the ability to fly with great ambition and conviction. Ballyhoo anticipated his daily sessions and was always keen to get going. The moment he was unhooded, he'd spot the kite, quickly rouse, then get on the wing. Stu heaped on plenty of praise for Ballyhoo's development, but he also kept me grounded and focused. Stu explained that I needed to understand the falcon is teaching itself how to navigate three vectors: (i) the weather, (ii) his ambition, (iii) his ability. It was important to teach myself how to condition him by varying the quality, quantity and moisture content of his food. This would ensure Ballyhoo was ambitious and capable of flying hard. I was producing that flickering dot and was beside myself imagining him folding at quarry.

After about four weeks, the kite had served its purpose. It was time to move on to the final phase in Stu's training regime. We needed to condition Ballyhoo so that he might fly in a manner that would put him within touching distance of a grouse, and earn him the prestigious title of 'gamehawk'.

*****

95

Gamehawk

The discipline of flying a gamehawk is taxing for a beginner. Without Stu's familiarity and experience upon which to draw, it would have been virtually impossible for me to correctly interpret Ballyhoo's efforts and intentions. Aside from increasing Ballyhoo's fitness, Stu's mentoring encouraged a desirable flying style, which enabled us to move into this final phase.

Until this point, Ballyhoo had only ever flown in a *pursuit* style. He remained standing on the fist until a target was presented to pursue (in his case a lure dangled from a kite string). Now, he needed to switch discipline. I needed to train Ballyhoo to fly in the manner of a gamehawk, stooping down from the heavens onto the quarry flushed beneath him. His target would be completely removed until he had completed the behaviour of 'waiting on' at a grand. His reward would be a covey of grouse to stoop – jack-pot.

A gamehawk has to fly in a waiting-on manner in order for the falconer to witness that dreamy stoop. Getting the falcon attuned to this style of flight requires progressive training. Mistakenly reinforcing or rewarding the falcon for not making criteria is a regressive action and can be of huge significance – greatly affecting the progress and consistency required to produce a gamehawk. By kite training for three to four weeks, Stu increased my chances of timing Ballyhoo's reward correctly. I could recognise the instant he exhibited desirable behaviour and, importantly, reward before distraction or exhaustion.

Ballyhoo's target would now be completely removed. The objective was to have him fly away from me promptly, with the ambition to gain height quickly, turn back and loyally wait on overhead for a reward. The only time Stu instructed me to offer a reward was when the falcon was achieving or had completed the session's objective. When enough sessions had passed, Ballyhoo should have learnt how to get success. He should repeat or improve upon his last performance, and would become that flickering dot. His jackpot for doing so would be flushed quarry on which to stoop.

Prior to waiting on, there is every opportunity for the gamehawk to become exhausted, distracted, to fly wide and lose command of the quarry. Producing the lure in any of these three situations is reinforcing and undesirable behaviour. Herein lies the quandary. At some point after the falcon leaves the fist, you have to recover it. The only way to do this involves you producing a lure for a recall (unless you pick her up on a kill). Therefore, when you present the lure needs to be timely and consistent with the training schedule, as well as how much feed you put on it,. It is the production of the lure or flushing quarry that are the primary reinforcing tools you have to shape and reward the behaviour. The falcon's level of anticipation enables progressive training.

Within your cooperative, the gamehawk needs to remain focused, busy-winged and loyal, whereas you need to provide the falcon with a reward and remain honest. You must be useful, but your presence must remain unassuming so that the falcon will fly upon its own conviction until the game is flushed or a garnished lure produced. You must never steal from or trick the falcon so that it finds you objectionable – fair exchange, no robbery. You must always be a useful, convenient, and timely servant.

Heading to the Highlands

Since the conception of *Peregrines over Pointers*, the meet evolved from a single day hawking larks with a merlin in lowland Suffolk to something more in line with Stu's vision. I pulled strings with some of my college gamekeeping contacts and, by good fortune, I found an estate willing to accommodate us for a week in the heart of the Cairngorms, Scotland. We were now in a position to pit our falcons against the acme of game birds over five days. It was time to make the stars align.

The excitement and anticipation became almost unbearable as we prepared for our adventure in the Highlands. It became impossible for me to fall asleep, infatuation and apprehension fuelling my insomnia. When my head hit the pillow, I could do nothing but dream of stoops and rakes. I'd imagine different scenarios that would send my heart racing as I agonised about all eventualities. At what point would I flush? How windy was too windy? How would Ralph Brown fair? Would I recall my falcon if he appeared outward or would I let him range? Would I fly in a downdraft? Was it sensible for me to trek solo in order to recover Ballyhoo should he fly off? What would I do if Ralph Brown got bitten by an adder? What if *I* got bitten by an adder!

Overthinking soon became a bit of a problem – one that would deprive me of many hours of sleep. I had to deliberately stop all thoughts of falconry otherwise my heart would race and I'd remain awake long into the night. Retired falconers, and those who are currently afflicted, say that obsessing over falconry starts with a slight exposure and quickly develops into a rage.

The dream of flying our peregrines over our pointers, hunting the most formidable of game birds in the splendour of the world's most beautiful landscapes, was soon to become a reality. Hollidge, Bishop and Stu loaded their chariots and began to venture north from East Anglia, up the A1, over the border and into the heart of the Scottish Highlands. Soon we'd be united with a profusion of pointers and peregrines, immersed in the grouse's kingdom.

We arrived at the bothy, our home for the next week. The pointers – my Ralph Brown, Stu's Shamrock (Sham for short), Hollidge's Dixie and Bishop's Bella – were as excited as anyone to be there. Before any unpacking could commence, we were compelled to give the dogs a run up the valley and let them reunite once more. Dixie, Bella and Sham were all siblings from Stu's bitch, Cody (daughter of Jess, with whom we hawked in the first Chapter). Cody had just been spayed after having her final litter, so it wasn't appropriate to bring her. Instead, Sham got the call-up. Other than Ralph Brown, the team were all English pointers bred by Stu. It was a strong squad to take into the Highlands to find grouse.

We returned the dogs to the vehicles so we could then decant the rest of our kit. It took a good hour or so to set up the weathering lawn, fill hawk baths, assemble dog crates and generally unload. It was thirsty work, too. The weather was unseasonably hot, and before long we were gathered in the glorious heat on the weathering lawn, quenching our thirst with my home brew, Wozale. I brewed the pale ale in The Box, its name deriving from traditional Christmas festivities, Wassail, and my nickname, Woz. We feasted and Wozaled into the late afternoon, the pointers walking amongst the falcons as they bathed, preened and relaxed into their new surroundings. We were here, finally, assembled on a small patch of grass and eagerly waiting for Monday's venture into the vast upland landscape. We stayed there until late afternoon, when the hungry midges forced us to withdraw.

We used Sunday to rest the falcons. This would enable us to bring their feeding time forward from late afternoon to midday. Our plan for Monday was to weather the falcons in the morning as we ate a hearty brunch, then take to the hill from about noon. My deliberating over what to feed Ballyhoo had me flustered. I was overthinking once more, and wondered if the down-time, warm temperatures and lack of flying would affect Ballyhoo's ambition. Should I make him a little more hungry to reduce the risk of him disappearing or would that prevent him from waiting on at a good height? I could not stop myself from overplaying scenarios and deliberating as I prepared his ration.

Having fed Ballyhoo and returned him to the weathering lawn by 12pm, I then paced the bothy, perturbed by what Monday would bring. Stu sat in the garden and smiled with every exhale of his cigarette each time I passed the open door. He recognised it all; Bishop and Hollidge too. The three of them were all seasoned pros, clear in their convictions about what they'd just fed their falcons. Their birds were simply returned to the lawn without any afterthought. Instead, these old timers talked nonsense, joked and relaxed as they sat watching the falcons bathe and preen. I was instructed by Stu to stop walking around and come sit in the sunshine. He said my needless patrolling was making the dogs nervous. Bishop handed me a can of Guinness, Stu threw a rolled cigarette in my lap, and Hollidge reminisced of stoops to distract me and send my heart racing. The stories, laughter and recollections of these old friends was the relaxing whale song I needed to keep cool.

My assumption of how four men would live in a bothy was one of surviving on beans on toast, ready meals and Guinness. How wrong I was. Hollidge made the kitchen his own, and a combination of hunger pains and a bottle of Sauvignon Blanc would see him set about his domain with incredible finesse and ferocity. During his time gamekeeping at Forsinard, Hollidge had been taught to cook game and red meats by a Belgian named Martillo. He specialised in cooking wild boar and other ungulates of the forest. Hollidge learned from his mentor and was now combining protein, carbohydrates and legumes to produce the most delicious red meat and game dishes I'd ever tasted. I thought I was proficient at cooking game from my time at Newbiggin Hall, salvaging the best cuts of roadkill and bowling pigeons out of the trees with my airgun, or from my time at The Box, reducing the honking bouquet of draft ewe to a safe level for consumption and making the mutton tender enough to eat with a spoon. No, Hollidge was on another level as he went through the kitchen riffing like a jazz drummer.

"Martillo, he must have been Michelin star, no?" I asked Hollidge, topping up his wine glass with an elegant £6.99 bottle of Sauvignon Blanc.

"I think the gun to the back of his head was more of an incentive to cook well, Dave," Hollidge replied whilst busily reducing his venison jus, having infused it with the blackcurrant jam I'd bought from the village shop. As he brought the gravy under control, Hollidge went on to explain that Martillo had been chef to Pablo Escobar, no less. The fact he made it out alive was testament enough of his ability to cook.

Martillo and Hollidge met in the early 1990s. Martillo fetched boar from the continent and traded these cuts of hog, along with his savvy chef skills, for Scottish stags and wild salmon taken from Hollidge's beat. On discovering this taste sensation, Hollidge produced his own feral swine of TamworthXwild boar cross-breed hogs to sniff the woodland of the estate and later be converted to chops, bacon and sausage.

That night we had an over-indulgence of moreish venison washed down with the last of the Wozale. Our conversation turned to paying homage to the grouse, *the* most formidable of all game bird species to pursue with a peregrine and pointer.

Why Grouse?

Red grouse live tough lives in a harsh and hostile environment. They certainly don't have it easy, having to contend not only with severely fluctuating weather in an exposed landscape, but also with a range of parasites and predators. As a means of avoiding the attentions of foxes, mustelids and birds of prey, grouse have remarkably camouflaged plumage, and a deeply ingrained impulse to move about unobtrusively. If spotted and forced into flight, however, they exhibit an astonishing turn of speed, and tenacious evasive behaviours – making them an awe-inspiring, fascinating and addictive quarry to pursue. Just a few hours of laying in the heather on the extreme uplands, detecting how the grouse nestles within the ecosystem, is sufficient exposure (save for the mosquitoes) to provide the itch that develops into further intrigue, stirred by this intrepid, resolute, keystone species.

©Amelia Siddle

The red grouse is endemic to the United Kingdom and, alongside the grey partridge, some species of waterfowl, migratory snipe and woodcock, form the native game-bird species of the British Isles. The non-native game birds prevalent in the U.K. include pheasant and red-legged partridge. That said, pheasants were probably introduced by the Romans in the first century and therefore are surprisingly more at home in the British countryside than, say, the potato, which arrived some 1600 years later.

Red grouse, pheasant and partridge are typically driven for the sporting gun. The grouse's significance as a standalone quarry species amongst these three is, however, unparalleled. The very fact that red grouse *cannot* be successfully bred in captivity and released is fundamental to its sporting elusiveness. By comparison, non-native pheasants and red-legged partridge breed readily. As a result, woodland, shelterbelts, and field margins can be oversaturated with unnaturally high populations of these two species. These lowland targets are therefore more convenient and plentiful to pursue, but alas, all lack the wild and elusive facets of the red grouse in its upland environment.

Heather moorland of the uplands is the only habitat able to support the red grouse. On a worldwide scale, Britain's upland expanses of open heather moorland are rarer than tropical rainforest. In spite of this, moorland is diminishing with changes in land use, particularly afforestation, overgrazing and wind-farming.

Where there are areas of suitable habitat, red grouse continue to remain fiercely independent, making the viability of establishing and maintaining a population that bit harder. This resolute and territorial game bird is determined to remain wild and self-sufficient, turning its beak up at supplementary feeding, man-made shelters and attempts to be coerced in captive-breeding programmes. To sustain and increase a population, it is necessary to preserve the habitat, rather than nurture the grouse.

The only superficial offering accepted by the grouse, believe it or not, is a complimentary handful of grit. Red grouse consume about 35 grams of grit each month. It is held in the gizzard to aid digestion of fibrous heather shoots, which account for 80 per cent of their diet. Such a rejection of hospitality forces the upland gamekeeper to ensure that all the other elements within the ecosystem required to sustain and increase the grouse population are present. This is a far cry from simply tipping a bag of release pellets into a pheasant feeder. Heather provides both ground nesting cover, and stems – upon which the grouse feeds. In addition, their diet will likely consist of buds from cotton grass, wild fruits such as blaeberry, cow and crowberry, and an abundance of insect life.

Grouse are very much at the mercy of parasitic infection (notably from nematode worms and ticks), weather anomalies and predation. The higher the density of grouse, the greater the effect the aforementioned can have on a population. A combination of poor habitat, predation, bad spring weather and disease will likely result in localised extinction. Red grouse have little ability to control parasitic infection. They do, however, exhibit innate behavioural characteristics to mitigate mild levels of predation present in a variety of forms, mammalian and avian. Pursuing such a revered species and such an appreciable escapologist is a rare privilege.

The red meat and Wozale made it impossible for me to lie awake and dwell. The next I knew of life was a rude awakening by whining pointers, impatient to get out at 5:30am. This marked the start of our first day. It began with us, rather worse for wear, taking the dogs for a quick hoon up the valley, then providing them with a light, early breakfast. Wearily, we filled the falcons' baths then placed them out to weather at 7:30am. By 8am we had what was probably our fourth or fifth cup of tea and were sitting watching the falcons warbling (stretching), rousing and preening as they took in the morning sunshine. As the guys kept an eye on the birds, I decided to sort breakfast. Spurred on by Hollidge's efforts the previous night, I par-cooked the sausages we'd bought from the local butcher, surrounded them with haggis and wrapped the lot with bacon before finishing them in the oven. My Scottish twist to pigs-in-blankets was the fuel required to get us up the mountains and sustain us until we came off the hill by late afternoon.

The dogs were beyond impatient watching us ready the falcons and fasten our hiking boots and gaiters. Stu packed into my Defender, Bishop into Hollidge's Discovery, then our convoy of two Land Rovers began to bumble up the rough single forestry access track. It took about 40 minutes, driving in low range and second gear, for us to ascend beyond the tree line to about 580 m above sea level. A big rock and turning circle marked the end of the access track and our place to alight. It was a stunning place, with the summits of steep-sided rocky Munros surrounding our hill range. The grey crags and mottled scree looked down on the rolling moorland of purple and brown where we stood. The in-bloom heather was interspersed with greens of lichens and sphagnum moss. There were wildflowers that made the place alive with bees, butterflies and insect life, and thankfully it was too hot and breezy for midges to amass. Looking up, we found a bright blue sky with occasional cirrus clouds passing through. It was a high-pressure scorcher. We'd yet to set off and already the dogs were all panting, so we filled dog bowls with drinking water for them to quench their thirst and stay hydrated.

We lifted the falcons out of the Land Rovers and checked their tracking devices. As the receivers were switched on in turn, the pointers all turned their heads in unison as the beeps from our receivers sang, charging the dogs' ambitions to be unleashed and find quarry. Stu and Bishop decided we should climb up the hill, a little further from the vehicles, in order to take in a big side of the hill that was facing into the wind. The slight updraft and thermals created by the wind would provide easy lift for the peregrines, but more importantly would make it easier for the falcons to remain focused and stay loyal.

Hollidge, Bishop and I stood in a huddle at the brink of the hill as Stu marched some 60 feet ahead of us, then paused. A long *peeeep* from his whistle was the command for Sham to drop, and Stu lifted the lead from around his neck. Sham lay tense in the heather. His eyes never averted from his master, who was busily readying Gilbert by removing her leash and swivel. Stu stood there for a few seconds, reckoning. Taking in the moment, Stu was motionless before slowly raising his right fist, then suddenly flicked his index finger. Taking his cue, Sham bolted off to the right, the wind at his cheek, throwing everything he had forward until he was about 80 metres from us. He then turned and came back towards us, almost cleaning our boots as he bound past, and ran about 80 metres out to our left. We watched on in a sense of heightened anticipation as he began to cover the ground. Sham's back legs tucked tight under his body then flexed forcibly rearwards, propelling him forward with incredible force. His front legs threw forward each bound, grounding and enabling his carriage to recycle. His was a phenomenal gate at a vehement pace. The spectacle was a far cry from the gentle giant who (yesterday) was basking in the sunshine and rolling on his back, lapping up our attention as we supped Wozale. Sham was now quartering the ground ahead of us, hunting with tenacity and flare in a style that he understood would please Stu.

Imagine your favourite rally car (mine is the Peugeot 205 T16), being driven at pace by the most skilful of drivers. The driver then performs a handbrake turn and skids the car round to a parked position, sending gravel spewing. Brittle heather stems, lichen and moss were the gravel to Sham's handbrake turn as he threw his body round and froze, nose to the wind, locked on a solid point. Stu, as before, paused and reckoned. This time he raised his left fist, averted his eyes from Sham and bit down on the hood brace. Using his right hand he struck the hood, then rolled it from the head of Gilbert.

There was a brief moment in which Gilbert remained motionless and withdrawn. Her eyes, like huge black marbles, now glistened in the sunlight as she held her head at different angles to scope the vast skies for threatening shapes. As she continued to look, her chest feathers began to swell. She nodded towards the direction of Sham, clocked our position, then returned to gaze once more at the horizon. Her crescendo to all this weariness was a huge rouse, culminating in her leaving Stu's fist and punching forwards and upwards. Gilbert continued this trajectory as Stu held his position. When she was at about 300 feet, Stu moved forward to advance the point. His aim was to circumnavigate the set-up to sandwich the grouse between himself and Sham. This movement would focus Gilbert and bring her overhead. Rather unfortunately, while making his arc, a single grouse, some distance from ones marked by Sham, flushed to Stu's left. Though she was far from occupying a commanding aerial position, Gilbert went after it like a rocket. The stoop was very shallow and nowhere near fast enough to catch the grouse, nevertheless, she rowed hard and was taken out of sight beyond the horizon in a matter of seconds. We waited for what could only have been a minute or so, but to me it seemed like half an hour. There was still no sign of Gilbert.

"I'll come with you Stu. I've got a mark of where she went over the horizon," I called, keen to help track her down. "Fuck that, I ain't going nowhere, yet," Stu replied, a little disappointed a grouse had bumped on his advance of the point. He knew that the likelihood of Gilbert having one over on the grouse was low but the last thing he wanted was to teach Gilbert to sit down somewhere and expect him to appear with food. Gilbert had to learn that the next best thing following a non-productive flight was to return and seek out Stu and the swung lure; so we waited. Nothing. No alarm calls from other wildlife. She had vanished. Stu unfolded his tracker and pointed it towards where she had crossed the horizon. It beeped, faintly. He left the tracker facing that direction and laid it in the heather. At least we had a fix on her, but she didn't appear to be moving. Might she have managed to grab the grouse? Doubtful. The faint beeps indicated it was quite a trek to the point where she had vanished, on energy-sapping terrain. I could tell Stu wasn't keen to get marching. He had a hunch and desperately didn't want to teach Gilbert to sit and wait for him. As Stu stood there swinging the lure, the receiver began to bleep louder and louder, marking the nearing of the transmitter. Hollidge then got eyes on Gilbert as she hugged the contours of the hill range and made her approach back to Stu's lure. Stu was delighted at her efforts. The flush had come at the wrong time, but Gilbert did all that was asked of her, and returned when unsuccessful. She was given a nice reward, and Stu had something positive to work with from her first day.

Stu rolled the hood back onto Gilbert and suggested I send Ralph Brown into a section of hill a little further down where a stream cut through the peat, and some wisps of cotton grass were visible. We could head towards the stream where the grouse might be dwelling, and if nothing came of it, we could at least get some water into the dogs. There was nothing for it but to send Ralph Brown into a good-looking patch of heather next to the stream. My trusty German went forth with great intention, but there was a marked difference between his running style and that of Sham's. I knew if he found anything he would point and flush on command, but the systematic quartering and neat covering of the ground ahead of us left a lot to be desired. Bang – he screeched to a halt. It was a solid point that he held. There must be something there, I thought. The ground looked perfect, and I had good faith in Ralph Brown. He was great at pointing pheasant and partridge on the low land, and grouse are a little more pungent. He was definitely locked on to game.

I drew a deep breath and unhooded Ballyhoo. It was something I'd done hundreds of times before, but this time it felt especially poignant. Ballyhoo left my fist and climbed forward. I could see him looking back at me with every circle he made, which I interpreted as him either being too hungry, or that he was unsure of himself. Nevertheless, he kept his wing beat and climbed easily on the natural lift to about 400 feet. Knowing he was on unfamiliar terrain, I moved forward to focus his attention and call the flush. I needed to teach him the lesson whilst I had the opportunity to be in control. This would set me up for the week ahead; eat-sleep-repeat. Ballyhoo was in a great position and, provided he pulled the trigger, was in a very commanding place, with every chance of getting close to the grouse. This was it.

"Get em up Ralph!" I yelled, and ran towards him with much excitement. Ralph Brown went in hard, and I expected a flurry of grouse to lift from the heather, only for a mountain hare to burst out. It turned sharply and ran straight up the hill, avoiding Hollidge, Bishop and Stu, onto a sheep track and away. Ballyhoo dipped a wing and moved out of position as he tracked the hare for a few seconds. He didn't commit to a stoop and remained waiting-on, his wings clipping away at a pacey rhythm. I went from extreme excitement to bitter annoyance, and looked over at Stu for some guidance. "Walk on a little further – the falcon should stay loyal. As soon as he's back overhead, reward him with the lure. He's flown great – don't push it." Stu was the voice of reason. I looked ahead of me to the stream. There was a slight embankment on the other side that led up to a softer, flatter area of cotton grass. From listening to the guys chattering over the weekend, I'd learned that not all brown (yearling) falcons like landing on heather. Some have a very strong aversion to touching the stuff and will fly until they find a suitable area to hold up. It is always advisable to engineer a flight so that young falcons get used to the heather, and various tactics can be deployed, such as landing a kit-rig or simply taking a dropped lure to eliminate the fear of heather. Not having had that luxury, I thought if I could cross the stream and get onto the clearer ground, I would make something out of the flight and end on a positive note – albeit an excruciatingly anti-climactic one.

Ralph Brown and I moved forwards. I sent him for a little skirmish and kept him as tight as possible to keep Ballyhoo's attention drawn towards us. It worked. As we made for the water, Ballyhoo tabbed overhead. I could capture his efforts by rewarding him with the lure. I just needed to jump the stream quickly and scramble up the embankment and get onto the nice patch of ground to bring him down safely. Ralph Brown and I leaped over simultaneously. I then looked up to recheck Ballyhoo was still with me. He was, and he looked awesome up there. He was an exciting flickering of gold and brown against the bright blue sky and I remember putting the disappointment of Ralph's unproductive find behind me and taking joy from seeing Ballyhoo showcase the exact behaviour I wanted from him. Even more pleasing was my ability to reinforce this. I resolved to deal with the anguish of the false start over a Wozale later that night. As I began to climb up and out of the ditch, my head levelled with the top of the bank and I could peer onto the flat ground where I was to drop the lure. To the side of me there was a sudden huge clatter. Ralph Brown must have disturbed an old cock grouse that had been hunkered in the hag, hiding under a small curtain of heather where the embankment undercut the plateau. It burst out from its hiding hole.

I was startled and stared at the grouse as it flew ahead of me. Before I could even think to look up and wonder where Ballyhoo was, or if he'd even acknowledge the flush, a dark streak flashed behind the grouse and raked it. The connection was so hard that the grouse bounced off the cotton grass. The impact was at eye level, right in front of me. Feathers plumed as Ballyhoo pillow-cased the grouse with a huge crump. Moss and other bits of vegetation were sent flying as the grouse rattled off the ground and, for a fleeting second, the water droplets spraying up from the sphagnum moss produced a tiny rainbow against the back-lit heather. Ballyhoo had inverted from his rake and was grasping the grouse in the heather, beak opened and panting hard.

It was all too much to digest, everything happened so quickly. We had each seen something of the flight the others hadn't. We gathered close and spent the time it took Ballyhoo to feast on his kill to recall in awe what we had seen. Hollidge remarked that Ballyhoo had exhibited the most desired characteristic for a grouse-killing tiercel: the hard hit and fast invert to bind to the prey. This was something he'd witnessed many times from Touchwood. Stu and I looked at each other and said nothing. Neither of us could stop smiling. I think we were both trying to work out who was more proud: him of me, or me of myself.

We were not too far from the vehicles. Having run our dogs and taken our flights, Stu and I elected to return to my Defender and offload, leaving us free to enjoy the other flights without burden. Whilst getting the dogs loaded into my truck, I tethered Ballyhoo to the large rock next to where we had parked, in order to free my hands. He looked fantastic there, all fed with a crop full of grouse. Stu announced that from now on we'd call the landmark 'Peregrine Rock'.

Bishop and Hollidge worked a lot of the ground ahead of them for no finds. Stu and I walked the track, and from the higher ground watched them each take in large beats with Bella and Dixie, taking it in turn to run then rest their pointers in the hot weather. The track came to a bend before dropping quite significantly and joining the woodland. This put a natural end to the beat, so we waited for our friends to catch up and were ready to congratulate them on their systematic dog work. Before they reached us, Bella snapped onto point; she was solid. Bishop unhooded his tiercel, which he had named Dude, raised his fist and cast him forward. Dude flew fairly close to Bishop for a while then began to track forward. Clipping away quite nicely, he flew over Bella then levelled with the drop-off and steeper slope. There he instantly found natural lift. Instead of beating his wings and being forced to work hard in the hot sun, Dude would turn and circle tightly on a fixed wing for intermittent periods as he used the thermal and slight breeze to go higher and higher. Peregrines get drunk on thermals and Dude had found the cocktail lounge. He was swooning in the updraft as he became smaller and smaller to the naked eye. Dude was outward and enjoying life on the wing and still ringing up; he was now just on the cusp of invisibility, the smallest black pixel against a bright blue sky. One after the other, each of us announced, "No, lost him." Luckily, Hollidge was no stranger to high-flying peregrines and was equipped with his 10x50 binoculars. He was the only one able to keep tabs on Dude in his carefree state.

Bishop needed to exercise some form of control. Failure to reign Dude in and keep focus would result in us losing him by distraction. Staying well back from Bella and the marked game, Bishop backed out of the set-up the way he had entered; this was the safest exit and the one least likely to spook the grouse. He took his lure from his pocket and swung it discreetly, to no effect. Dude remained fixed-winged and happy to remain wide at terrific altitude.

Bishop made it up to the track and started walking towards Stu and me in an attempt to circumnavigate the point. He wanted to get ahead of the set-up and use the lure to bring Dude overhead. Bishop's movement was enough of a stimulus to eventually get Dude's attention, and Hollidge shouted that he was tabbing back towards us. With his wings half-tucked, Dude began gliding over, almost in a very shallow stoop, lowering his altitude until we could get eyes on him once more. He had lost a lot of height in moving to our location from what must have been at least a kilometre away. Not wanting Dude to lose any more height and recall, Bishop hid his lure and stood still. On hiding the lure, Dude slowly came across the skyline towards us to put himself in a position where Bella could flush. He was still well over a grand, but in flying over towards us he hit the same thermal he found at the beginning of his flight. Like your boozy mate who slips back into the pub for another pint, Dude was back in the cocktail lounge, and once more began to ascend on fixed wings. Bella had been on point now for at least 15 minutes. In fact, she'd laid down but was still fixed and marking the game. Dude stayed on the thermal and would soon be out of sight for a second time. As Dude ascended, Bishop moved closer towards us, then produced his lure once again. The set-up was pretty good. Bella was hunkered down marking the grouse. She was sandwiched by Hollidge on one flank, and the three of us on the other. The reemergence of the lure was sufficient to reign Dude in, and he was more reactive to it. He lost a bit of height but was coming over quite quickly. As soon as Dude had passed overhead of Hollidge, Bishop called to Bella and triggered the flush. Bella rushed in and a covey of five grouse burst from the heather, looking to clear the moor. In doing so, they flew right past the three of us! Dude transformed from fixed-wing to closed teardrop. He was a black missile that tore after the covey and ripped the sky into whistling ribbons as air screamed through his leg bells. The grouse hugged the contours of the hill and headed over a sharp gorge. We watched this shrieking blur level then bound to one of the grouse over the valley. Feathers exploded to the sound of bells ringing, and the pair crashed into the side of the cut.

"He's hit it, he's bound!" I yelled. It was one of the most amazing stoops and spectacles I'd seen. Once more, we gathered in while the falcon ripped into his prize. Much fuss was made of Bella as I told Bishop about 'Peregrine

Rock'. Bishop was adamant that Dude should have his own landmark for that epic flight, and proclaimed a boulder on the side of the track as 'Dude's Bolder'. Already we were beginning to add markers to our Ordnance Survey map, and make lasting memories.

We'd run out of moor on this particular beat. Hollidge looked at his watch and calculated that by the time Dude had fed and we had walked back to the vehicles, the window of opportunity to fly his falcon, Molly, would have passed. She was already exhibiting signs of hunger. Hollidge elected to simply feed his falcon to keep her focused and set for tomorrow. Dixie had done a lot of running and he didn't want to push her. We all agreed he'd be first in the chair tomorrow, and drew the day to a close.

In the hope that I might have caught a grouse, I had packed a couple of nice bottles of wine in order to toast Ballyhoo – drinks were on me. It was Bishop's turn to cook, so he shot off the moor and into town to gather the supplies. We were all in high spirits back at the bothy. The camaraderie in our collective could not have been any more joyful and we were looking forward to our next falconers' feast. The dogs were shattered and sleeping in their crates despite the crashing of pans and baking trays coming from Bishop's efforts in the kitchen. Bishop was on a culinary mission, so we stood outside admiring the falcons as they bathed and preened on the weathering lawn.

"Five minutes, boys," Bish shouted from the kitchen.

That was quick, I thought to myself – he's barely been in there for half an hour. I went to the Welsh dresser, lifted four large wine glasses and filled each one with a healthy slug of Châteauneuf-du-Pape, a wine far beyond my pay grade. Be that as it may, this was a special occasion and a fitting aperitif. We gathered outside on the lawn to toast the falcons: Ballyhoo and Dude with their bursting crops, Gilbert and Molly carrying the weight of expectation for tomorrow. Bishop nipped back inside to serve up dinner before calling us through. We carried our wine through to the table and were greeted with cold, packet ham from the co-op, served with egg and chips.

It turns out Bishop really can't cook, but what he lacks in culinary skill, he makes up for in trying. Not only was this the sum of what he could muster, but he explained it was on the fancy end of the spectrum. Bishop had pushed himself and managed two eggs each, with runny yokes and crinkle-cut chips. He would never live it down:

ham, egg, and chips avec le Châteauneuf-du-Pape.

We were up bright and early once more. As expected, Ballyhoo and Dude were vastly overweight from gorging on grouse, so Bishop and I elected not to fly. Instead, we fed quarter rations and left our boys behind. We were both keen and excited to see Gilbert and Molly take to the air. Both falcons were about on-weight, so we headed to the moor nice and early. The weather was a bit blustery and there was a storm coming, so Stu and Hollidge were eager to get going. Hollidge was first up with Molly, his big and very capable peregrine falcon. Molly had a good few seasons under her belt and she was wise to gamehawking. It didn't take long for Dixie to secure a point, and Molly was soon in the air commanding the point. Molly stayed loyal and was eager for the flush. She had no ambition to fly beyond about 400 feet and was looking inward – maybe she was a touch too hungry. Hollidge waited until the exact moment she was focused and directly overhead before calling for the flush. Dixie raced a few paces forward and produced three grouse. The powerful and seasoned Molly made short work of the stoop and knocked one of the grouse hard into some long heather. The momentum of the rake carried her past the point of impact and she lost sight of her prize buried in the long, rank heather. A dusting of grouse feathers gave us a marker of where the bird had gone down. Hollidge and Dixie went to investigate and quickly recovered the grouse, whose neck was broken. It was killed instantly on impact. Hollidge then threw it onto a patch of shorter heather, and Molly could come down to feast.

Sham had to run a good distance to find the next point, but in the cooler conditions he was more than up for the task. As soon as he scented the grouse he was locked on point. With the confidence that Gilbert would more than likely chase and, more importantly, recall, Stu got Gilbert into the air and took his time. Gilbert had a similar flight to Molly. She stayed quite loyal and expectant, so instead of heading the point and risk bumping grouse again, Stu decided to move as close as he dared to Sham and waited patiently until Gilbert flew overhead. She was still quite inward, and at about 400 feet she punched directly overhead – at which point Stu clicked his fingers. Responding to the click, Sham moved forwards and burst a covey of grouse, which shot off down the glen. Gilbert held a short stoop before singling one out, and powered after it. This wily grouse wasn't in any mood to be outdone by a young peregrine. It jinked superbly and dumped into some long heather, sending Gilbert flying past only to look back to where the grouse had disappeared. It was enough to reward her for. "If she keeps progressing like that, she'll get the right one under her," Stu remarked as he started swinging his lure.

Gilbert came haring back in and recalled instantly, to Stu's delight. "I can feed her well for that," Stu said as he sat down in the heather. He fed Gilbert on the fist and made plenty of fuss over Sham. I watched on, admiring how the three of them bonded, content in their hunting cooperative: man, peregrine and pointer. It was within this trio of unlikely bedfellows that Stu was most absorbed. His relaxed demeanour was derived from developing several gamehawks and countless flights. Success, for Stu, wasn't about the kill. It was about developing and achieving the spectacle, the aesthetic, and being fully immersed in this calmed affiliation. Stu had witnessed countless phenomenal flights that didn't result in a kill, but bloody nearly did. He took as much joy in the *bloody nearlies* as he did in the flights when quarry was taken.

The Wednesday and Thursday of the tour proved to be a bit of a mixed bag. The moorland deities must have felt we'd been overly blessed on our first two days and decided to call us into check. Wednesday was far too stormy, and Thursday saw the hill range blanketed by fog. On our final day, Stu pulled me aside at the morning weigh-in. He warned me that I needed to do Ballyhoo justice and not fail him. Ballyhoo was still learning, and I needed to cement the lesson in his head. There were two things I needed to do to achieve this: first, guarantee quarry under him, and second, produce it at the right time.

"Fly over Sham, and let me call the flush," Stu insisted. I think he could sense that my exuberance had all the hallmarks of a cock-up. Stu didn't want me to make a rookie error and felt it necessary to exercise some control. Of course, I agreed. We set off close to the vehicles. I kept Ralph Brown on lead and Stu sent Sham forth. Sure enough, he was quick to secure a point. Stu looked at me, nodded and told me to fly it. Ballyhoo left my fist and quickly ascended to half a grand, and I called for the flush. Stu ignored my instruction, instead he watched Ballyhoo. "Now Stu," I shouted and ran towards him, thinking we needed to get the grouse in the air.

"Stand still!" Stu shouted as loud as he dared. I froze, frustrated he didn't flush.

"We ruined it," I exclaimed.

"He's a little too wide. Just wait," Stu briskly replied, shutting me down as he watched Ballyhoo pull off and continue to beat his wings. His motion took him to about 750 feet, then he began to tab back over the top of us and look inward once more. "We'll go this time, get ready," Stu said, as he waited a little longer, patiently orchestrating the whole thing. I looked up at Ballyhoo at the exact moment Stu clicked his fingers. Sham nudged forward and froze, Stu clicked again, and Sham went in and produced the flush.

Ballyhoo held a tight stoop and tore after the grouse as they shot off down the glen. The grouse were rapid in their bid to clear the moor and make good their escape. They took him over a ridgeline and out of sight. He was some distance behind the grouse but did appear to be gaining on them. Thinking he was going to be unsuccessful, I took out my lure and stood waiting to see him reappear. The tracker was indicating he was still, and in the direction of a rocky outcrop that curved around the ridgeline. I convinced myself he was sitting somewhere on the rocks out of sight of me and the lure. Stu rolled a cigarette as I set off in the direction of the scree. As I levelled with the rocks and made my way further around the hill, I began to make out the faint clinking of bells. *Jingle-jingle*, nothing, *jingle-jingle*, nothing. Sure enough, as I homed in on the sound, I found Ballyhoo was plucking his grouse, each motion sending the bells into a momentary frenzy. Then there was silence as he froze and checked the skyline. Hollidge had his trusty 10x50s trained on me. I was fist pumping, and they realised Ballyhoo was on a grouse.

Stu recalling Sham 📷©Leopold Amory

This was the most remarkable flight of the day. Whilst I was ecstatic, I was also eating humble pie, and bowed to Stu's experience. The others had good flights, but the grouse won on every occasion. We packed up the bothy and loaded our vehicles, saddened that the week had come to an end. We had enjoyed such an adventure, witnessed a truly awesome stoop and had been given a taste of what the moor had to offer – excitement, anguish, jubilation. Experiencing the complexities of this discipline and being with Stu, Hollidge and Bishop had given me plenty of opportunities to learn. Now it was time for me to reflect on the week of grouse hawking and leave this landscape to its custodian, the upland keeper.

*****

The Upland Game Keeper

The upland keeper is no socialite. Theirs is a profession at odds with working time directives, and certainly void of trade union representation. The lifestyle choice offers only the slightest of respite against the relentless obligations brought about by the change of the seasons and the cover of night-fall. There is no way of cheating your way to success. Being poorly skilled, ill-informed, or with little motivation to forge over rugged landscape in any weather, will quickly give rise to failure. These attributes are a definite prerequisite to stay clear of the vocation.

Owning the title Gamekeeper requires a certain strength of character. Once a position of authority and respect, in modern times the job title is villainised with criminal rhetoric, rather than championed as a proponent of conservation or the management of rare habitat. The advent of gunpowder, followed by a fashion for shooting spurred by Queen Victoria's love of the Highlands, marked a watershed moment for all predators that might pose a threat to gamebirds. At the height of the so-called 'Balmorality' era of the mid-19th century, nothing with pointed teeth or a hooked bill was safe from the army of gamekeepers who patrolled the country estates. These days, necessary predator control continues. And in isolated instances perpetrated by a minority of individuals, illegal persecution of species protected by the Wildlife and Countryside Act occurs. Some species are affected more than others. Large raptors, including the hen harrier and iconic golden eagle, have most recently been brought to the fore – their poisoned bodies recovered and mysterious disappearances tracked thanks to data provided by satellite tagging. Of course, raptors face other threats, some more widespread than poison or bullet. Agricultural intensification, prey scarcity, wind farms, land use and climate change are arguably of more existential significance, but you are unlikely to see the anti-grouse-shooting fraternity shed as much light on this, nor chastise the farmer and forester as they berate gamekeepers.

Perhaps you have little sympathy, but do be aware of the Law of Unintended Consequences. Consider, for example, what would happen to all that habitat in the absence of sporting interest. It is likely the owner will convert the precious heather moorland to commercial forestry. Most species will be unable to penetrate the dense, monoculture timber stands, and the rich fauna finds itself unable to thrive. The numbers of corvids, foxes and mustelids would rise precipitously, and protection from these nest-raiding predators removed. It has been demonstrated that unmanaged and abandoned moorland suffers a decrease in biodiversity, and the most detrimental effects are seen on the rarer species; ring ouzel, dotterel, golden plover, black grouse, capercaillie, ptarmigan, Eurasion curlew, northern lapwing, merlin, all owl species, and mountain hare – to name a few that so many conservation initiatives are at great pains to protect.

Gamekeepers are exceptional operatives for species conservation. Conservation is not simply a case of putting a fence around a bit of ground with the expectation that the encircled land will become a wildlife haven for rare, red-listed species. The art to conservation is simply deciding what species or habitat you wish to preserve, then to guard against a multi-faceted enemy that threatens your success. Upland keepers do exactly this, working for a real-term pittance with a grafting ethic that would put any field worker to shame.

✎©April Coppini

When we look at managing the health of moorland, it is necessary for the upland keeper to take a microscopic view, beyond fauna and flora. Disease and parasitic infection will wreak havoc on any species population that dwells there – none more so than the red grouse. The most taxing element of the keeper's responsibility is not necessarily to fill the crow trap, but to decrease the devastating effects of disease and parasites, mostly:

(i) Strongylosis: a disease brought by an overpowering presence of the strongyle worm. The larvae slither up the shoots of heather, on which the grouse depends and feeds. Once ingested, the larvae grow into visible threadworms, and will feast until their host can no longer support them.

(ii) Sheep tick: a parasitic arachnid that ascends foliage and awaits a passing host, to which they attach themselves and feed. Because they cannot choose which hosts they will encounter, ticks are decidedly unfussy, and will feed on just about any vertebrate that walks, crawls or slithers past them – including grouse. The actions of the tick allow for micro-parasites to be transmitted from one host to the next. Louping ill (see below) is of most consequence for grouse, but ticks also pass Lyme disease, babesiosis and anaplasmosis to humans.

(iii) Louping ill: a viral infection that attacks the nervous system. It will survive in a variety of hosts that dwell in the highlands, including deer, horses, grouse, hare and sheep. Although prevalent, it will rarely kill hare or ungulates, but may kill up to 60 per cent of infected sheep, and, even more alarmingly, up to 80 percent of infected grouse. For sheep there is a vaccine, but more importantly (and of huge significance for the upland keeper) there is also a contact treatment that will kill the tick as soon as it feeds on the sheep. This makes controlled shepherding one of the best defences against prolific tick burden and high prevalence of Louping ill on the moor.

The optimum canvas for a healthy moor is a mosaic of heather, cotton grass and *Vaccinium* berries. A variety of growth stages within the heather is the overriding factor responsible for increasing biodiversity and the population growth of all fauna. To achieve this, patches of the older, shin-length heather is burnt; this should account for approximately one sixth of the total volume of heather of the moor, leaving five sixths of the moor covered in heather, which varies in growth stages between emerging shoots and shin-length heather. Burning will also kill the heather beetle, *Lochmaea suturalis*. This beetle has a devastating effect on heather, reducing wide regions of healthy moorland to ash-grey deserts.

The idea that the management of sporting uplands only benefits aristocrats wanting to blast grouse is a grand misconception. Enjoyment is massively skewed in favour of those not holding a shotgun, all gladly wanting inclusion and submersion in the camaraderie, humour and kinship amongst like-minded, congenial folk.

Everyone retires in great spirits to the hostelry or homestead. In their hands may be a brace for the pot, in their pocket a cash-filled envelope. Wax jackets hang next to the fire, usually adjacent to wet socks. Exhausted dogs lie next to the flames, motionless except for deep breathing, long stretches and excited woofs as they dream of flushing game and retrieving quarry to hand – a nirvana for the lucky few, sadly unknown by many.

*****

The Bleak Midwinter

The phone rang one early December evening. It was Stu. "Something's come up, Dave. I've made arrangements. You're going to take on a bitch from my last litter." Stu then went on to explain that this puppy was his choice bitch and was gifted to someone subject to breeding obligations. Unforeseen circumstances now meant she had been returned to him. "She's a year old, house-trained, but knows nothing of game. Don't worry, that's all in the breeding, I'll teach you all you need to know." There was a long pause as Stu waited for all this to sink in.

"Hang on Stu, I've got Ralph Brown. I'm not looking for another dog, not least a second-hand pointer pup." I couldn't look past my boy, Ralph Brown. Besides, I had no space for another dog. I lived in a small cottage with Dobson, and we were certainly not at home to a crazy pointer puppy reject. Stu's forthright assumption that he could place a dog into my hands didn't sit easily with me.

"I don't want anyone else to take her, you've got to have her. You need to trust me on this, Dave. Let her get to know you then I'll talk you through everything you need to know when it's time for the moor." Stu was adamant. In the heat of the moment, I felt I had little choice, so I took a leap of faith on his choice bitch. She was a sweet lemon-and-white pointer with beautiful markings. The fact she was very excitable, jumpy and a lemony colour meant I decided immediately to change her name to Roo, after the young kangaroo in A. A. Milne's *Winnie the Pooh*. Roo and Ralph Brown got on famously, and so we settled in for a dark, dreich winter in The Box.

The long winter evenings gave Dobson and me plenty of time to reflect, and regret failing to collect enough firewood to fill the log store. Typically, Dobson would train each evening on the running track, so I would usually be first home to The Box, where the indoor temperature barely made double figures. I became proficient at lighting a fire from wet timber having spent hours kneeling in front of a pathetic effort, adding fuel and using Dobson's set of antique bellows in a bid to get some heat into the place. The hissing of damp wood would serve to mock me as wafts of smouldering pine escaped the cold draw of the chimney and rolled across the ceiling to meet the frosty windowpanes. To many people, this sounds miserable, but we both actually quite liked it. An evening spent pitting our wits against a reluctant fire was an alluring challenge, rewarded with a slow warming of feet, flames to stare at, and thick woollen jumpers that smelt of campfire smoke. We kept ourselves in good spirits drinking plenty of leaf tea and sloe gin.

As Christmas neared, I disappeared for a whistle-stop visit to Stu and Mandy's. Not only did they have central heating, but Stu had free-lofting chambers in which we would over-winter our peregrines. The short winter days – few of them fair – made it increasingly difficult to hunt or exercise our falcons. In such situations, it is best to take the falcons off tether and house them in secluded aviaries, allowing them to bulk up and moult. Being the furthest south of our two locations, housing the falcons at Stu's meant they would receive increased daylight hours and higher temperatures sooner – putting them several weeks ahead in their moult, compared to housing them in Scotland.

It was great to be sitting in Stu and Mandy's kitchen once more. Roo was beside herself to be back in her natal home, and received plenty of fuss from her mother, Cody. The evening was filled with much warmth and banter. The following morning, we cleared the aviaries of leaves, pressure washed them and disinfected all the perches, and replaced the pea-gravel substrate. The falcons were cut free from the leather anklets and ribbons that held the radio trackers secure. They then underwent a few simple husbandry interventions. Their beaks were trimmed, they were wormed, and received a quick mist of anti-mite spray across their feathers. There was nothing for it but to place them in the aviary and shut the door on them, leaving us to chat about all the *bloody nearlies* and reflect on the rest of the season.

The following morning, after having checked the peregrines, we had bacon, eggs, toast and plenty of tea before I got on the road and made the six-and-a-half-hour journey home. I was pleased to have made it back before dark. On this occasion, Dobson's car was parked outside The Box and there was smoke coming from the chimney. I walked into the kitchen and shouted through to the living room. "I'm making tea, did you struggle getting the fire started with that wet oak?" The familiar voice of an unruffled scientist replied, "Not at all. I had some Christmas cards arrive today which, when added to all of yours, provided excellent kindling – no better use for them." I peered round the corner – he was joking, right? Dobson looked up from the hearth and shrugged his shoulders. His eyebrows wore their typical logical frown, which read *don't attempt to argue. Instead, admire all this space I've made on the mantelpiece, and the nice warm fire we have.*

Later that evening, as was normal, I was stitching a hood while Dobson sat in his Chesterfield, shaking his head whilst scrawling on some paper – his legs stretched out towards the fire. I was mistaken for thinking Dobson was marking one of his students' theses. Instead, I was surprised to learn it he had taken it upon himself to peer review an edition of *The Watchtower*. "Had some lovely Jehovah's Witnesses catch me as I got home from the track, didn't really have time to chat but I took their flyer and invited them back to go through it next week." The steam rising from Dobson's wet athletics socks chased the smoke up the chimney while he plotted the evolutionary origins of the bacterial flagellum motor, thus providing an alternative to *The Watchtower's* inference that its discovery can be hailed as proof of creation. "I'll write this up for them, using my typewriter," Dobson announced, looking at me facetiously, seeking my approval.

I was stitching a neck band on a Dutch hood, when I became distracted by Dobson *clack-clacking* busily on his Underwood typewriter. Having looked up, my concentration returned to the room, and I noticed Ralph Brown was not curled with Roo in front of the fire. Instead, he had slunk off to the back door, where I found him hunched and looking directly down, his muzzle just inches from the doormat. Big licks of saliva dribbled from his mouth and pooled on the mat. 'Ralph, go on out then," I said, thinking he'd maybe eaten too much grass and needed to throw up. When I opened the door, he made no attempt to move, even when the door swung into his side. Expecting there would be a dirty protest on the front mat very soon, I lifted him outside and placed him on the grass. Ralph Brown stood motionless, holding the same hunched position. His tail, which had been a waggy blur only half an hour ago, was pulled down tightly between his legs. After a few moments, he began to shiver. I knew what this meant so I quickly reached for the phone and dialled my vet. "Hello, Dave. What can I do for you at this time of the night? Dave, are you there?" I found that I was suddenly rendered speechless as my brain acknowledged the gravity of the situation. My jaw locked rigid. I knew that my shocked state was wasting precious seconds, but I was dumbstruck watching Ralph Brown begin to sway a little. I wanted to reply to the vet, but was struggling to get my voice.

"I am, my dog – my dog needs help." That was as much as I could muster. I was choked and in a broken state. Sensing the seriousness of it all, he simply said, "Ok Dave, get to the practice, I'll meet you there."

Putting Ralph in the back of the Land Rover, I could hear the haunting sounds of my boy whining in pain. His breathing was sharp, shallow and laboured. Dobson drove. Not only had I had a good helping of sloe gin earlier, I wanted to be in the back and holding Ralph Brown. The diesel engine drowned out Ralph's whimpers but couldn't silence my frantic thoughts. I knew this was bad, and a sense of the inevitable was growing stronger. We arrived at the practice ahead of the vet, switched off the engine, and opened the boot of the Land Rover. The streetlamps of the adjoining road shone across the car park and shed just enough light for me to see Ralph. His gaunt eyes now stared deep into mine as I sat and held his inflamed body, stroking his ears. I couldn't speak to him. I wanted to, but my throat was pained, paralysed. I was scared that if I did speak, my pained tones would not serve to comfort Ralph. I knew, we both knew, that this was goodbye.

I wanted to be strong for him. As I tried to keep him still, Ralph lifted his head and started licking my hand. There he was, dying in my arms, yet he was doing his damnedest to reassure me – perhaps to thank me, even? I don't know. He pawed at my arm, digging his claws into my wrist and dragging me close, continuing to lick my hand as I stroked his ear.

When the vet opened the car door, it was impossible for me to speak to him. I didn't think anything needed to be said as he slid his stethoscope over Ralph's barrelled gut. He confirmed my suspicions. "It's a prolapsed gut." As soon as he said it, I just forced the words out. "I know, hurry." The vet returned to the car with a syringe in his hand. "This will take all his pain away. He'll become very drowsy, then be fast asleep. Stay with him, then once he's asleep, walk away and I'll come back and put him to rest."

Ralph stayed at rest in the back of the Land Rover until the following morning. I decided I would bury him on the large hill range that overlooked The Box. Ralph knew that hill like the back of his paws. There were always curlews, pheasants and hares for him to scent up there and, if his spirits rose a little higher, a grouse moor beyond the ridge to keep him amused. I found comfort in knowing all I had to do was look out of the cottage window onto the hill to embrace his memory.

The outlook was as dreich as the weather. I looked at the crags and readied myself to bury my Ralph Brown. The rain and bitterly cold wind made Dobson and I purposeful as we gathered some tools; the sensation of gripping the freezing spade and pinch bar was as unwelcome as the task in front of us. We got into the Land Rover and drove as high up the hill as possible, finding a sheltered section of hillside near a dry stone wall. Dobson and I began to dig. It was hurried and a little frantic, but I tried to keep my mind focused on the cut of the spade through the peat, the clang of rock, the depth of the growing hole. Anything to keep from thinking about the next step. I knew if I paused now, I'd crumple. Doing my best to put off the inevitable, I thumped on downwards. Dobson had to stop me. Putting his hand on my arm he said, "It's enough. Come on."

Ralph was still curled in the same position in the Land Rover as when he'd passed. I lifted him out and gently laid him to rest. We began to cover him over. I supressed my emotions and continued the task in a purposeful manner until the grave was full. Dobson and I then picked a large flat flagstone and, with considerable difficulty, laid it on top. I took the bottle of sloe gin from the front seat and tipped a good splash onto his grave before bringing the bottle to my lips. As I exhaled, I remember being quite surprised at how well I had held my composure. My throat was raw and eyes tear-shot, but I was not beyond function, and certainly not the inconsolable mess I had imagined I would be. Neither Dobson nor I could bring ourselves to say any words. Nor did we need to. There was nothing useful to be said.

The weather was unrelenting, so after a brief moment of reflection, we threw the tools in the back of the Land Rover and began the descent. I hadn't even got out of first gear, bumbling down off the hill in the Land Rover, before the full force of emotions hit me. I had to stop as I slumped in the seat and sobbed, really sobbed. There was an incomprehension, a misfiring; I couldn't understand coming off the hill without Ralph Brown. I'd never left him behind – we had been inseparable for 10 years and we had always gotten home safely together. Leaving your dog on the hill is something you never ever do. It took all that I had to engage first gear and drive back to the cottage without him.

Ralph Brown 📷©Dave Warren

By Endurance, We Conquer

The spring equinox passed, and the sun that had been absent from our cottage throughout the winter began to peak over the Burnfoot hill range so that we were no longer cast in a frozen shadow. Firstly, our windswept chimney pot would glimmer as the mid-afternoon rays of sunshine shone over the crags, then, a few weeks later, the entire larch cottage would creak and stir like a creature gently venturing from hibernation as the sun rose a little higher in the sky to mark the spring of 2015. Grief, too, was easing its grip, though I couldn't help but reflect on the time I'd spent with Ralph Brown.

I am convinced there is additional sentiment, an increased connectivity that compounds the loss of a working dog over any other. This may sound highly offensive to those who've experienced sorrow at losing a pet, but those who have experienced losing a working dog (guide, service, military or gundog) would concur it is a much deeper, gut-wrenching sorrow having been the recipient of the servitude and loyal purpose working dogs provide their handler. Once Ralph Brown was in his grave, only then did I fully appreciate that not only was he a great companion who I loved dearly; he gave me his all. He gladly threw his body on the line as soon as his paws hit the dirt, with unquestioning conviction, in order to work and find game for me. He understood his purpose and my intention, and would forge on to fulfil his part of the operation. Our partnership went deeper than simply enjoying a nice walk in the park or a run on the beach. In understanding this, I became ever more grateful as Roo yearned for interaction and stimulus. She ensured that falling into a depressive recumbency was impossible for me as we shaped our new partnership. I became accepting and was no longer so mournful. Instead, I kept progressing with Roo's training under Stu's guidance. She was shaping up nicely, though I could tell she missed Ralph Brown. Roo would often expect him to appear, and each time was a heart-wrenching moment, looking in her confused eyes and half-tilted head attempting to convey *'he won't be back.'*

I was also settling into an earthly rhythm. Exposure to the wilds around this time shifted my tempo from an overly exuberant and impatient enthusiast into a more reflective student of hawk and hound. I was hugely influenced by the nature of my relaxed mentor, Stu. Springtime, for the falconer, is the time to lift the foot off the gas, to enjoy having the falcons away in their chambers, cool off and allow the rage to subside.

Seasons keep the falconer balanced and regulate their wellbeing. When a first-year bird is returned to the safety of the aviary in the winter, the clock that marks time begins in the month of April. The minute hand creeps forward at approximately 0.2 mm per hour – matching precisely the speed at which feathers grow. Each rotation sees an old flight feather shed from the falcon and a new one begin to grow in the follicle. Firstly, the odd secondary feather alights, then the principal feathers are cast in sequence. Both wing and tail feathers moult from innermost to outermost, in symmetry from the body towards the extremities. Typically, the centre deck feathers of the tail are the first main flight feathers to drop, and the leading edge or number one primary wing feather is the last to be replaced.

As the watched kettle never boils, nothing is gained from observing the slow-paced transition of a falcon completing their moult. Everything is to be gained from patience as it morphs from a brown, juvenile bird to one that has sub-adult or fully mature plumage. Moulting is nature's way of ridding disfigured feathers that would otherwise permanently disable aerial prowess. The juvenile plumage that may have granted yearling birds ease of passage when negotiating adult territories is thrown to the ground and replaced with a jacket that invites altercation and evokes fear. During the moult, worn, shard, dry feathers give way to lush, waxy, vibrant plumage. Snapped tips are replaced by pin-perfect edges. Mottled becomes distinct, splodges become inky licks, toes and ceres turn from slate blue to dusky yellow, the tail length shortens.

Watching brown falcons lose their juvenile pyjamas and grow adult plumage is a slow-release drug of anticipation. Falconers ghost walk round their aviaries, switching between spy holes in order to satisfy their desire to keep tabs on changes in appearance. These answers are drip-fed to the compulsive Peeping Tom over the course of about four months. This is a fraught period in which the falconer is exasperated by the knowledge that any disturbance will result in fret marks on feathers, or worse, a snapped feather.

Stu warned that the head must rule the heart when it comes to reclaiming the falcons from the aviary. It was fitting that he was in charge, otherwise I would have likely become too eager and taken up the falcons before they were ready. Eventually that phone conversation came, and Stu invited me down in late July to reclaim Ballyhoo. I was desperate to see what he looked like now. The road trip to Cambridge was hotly anticipated, I looked forward to getting into Stu's kitchen and soaking up the ambiance. As when we first collected the falcons from Hollidge, Stu had fasted the birds for 24 hours, but on this occasion, I was able to peer into the aviary before we caught them up. Ballyhoo had gone through quite a transition, from brown and mottled to inky blue, black and slate grey. He was handsome and looked bigger and far more defined than I remembered. I couldn't wait to get him on the fist or to see him blocked-out on the lawn. He looked very striking with an oily rich head and a marked orbital ridge, which gave him a commanding frown. Stu caught up both birds in the aviary and held them as I attached their kit. We then wetted them and blocked them out on the lawn next to their baths. Having experienced life out of the aviary the previous season, they were steady enough to be placed on their perches and have their hoods removed. So long as we didn't bother them, they would soon settle, which gave us the excuse to drink tea and marvel at them from a distance as they dried and preened.

The moor was booked for the first week in September. This gave us four-and-a-half weeks to get the peregrines into shape. Reclaiming a pre-trained falcon is quite a mechanical affair. Ballyhoo was accepting of his surroundings and the inquisitions of Roo, however he was very stubborn and unwilling to respond to the routines of flying until he'd regained his appetite. He didn't require desensitisation so much, but I needed him to show a desire and confidence to respond to the lure. It took about two weeks of reduced food intake for Ballyhoo to diminish his fat reserves and get a strong appetite – strong enough to focus and fly unequivocally for food. As soon as we crossed that point, we were off. The creance (training line) lost its use after three days, and I knew he was ready to fly without tether once more.

Technology has come a long way. Somewhere around the world, a falconer had taken the initiative to ditch the kite and use a drone to raise the lure high into the sky. There are marked differences, but on the whole, the gadgetry pros outweighed the cons, so I introduced Ballyhoo to the flashy quadcopter without much objection. The main consideration is that the drone is not connected to a ground anchor, so, on snatching the lure, the falcon can't slide down a rigging to your feet. Instead, the lure is attached to a parachute, and as the falcon pulls the lure, the sail falls from the drone and the falcon comes parachuting in free fall down to the ground – which in itself has logistical implications. As the drone operator, you have to place the drone upwind in the sky to allow for the correct trajectory to land the falcon in the same field in which you are standing. The drone can't be flown in strong winds and for more than about 15 minutes, so if the falcon is slow off the mark, has a very slow climb rate, sits or is distracted, the drone has to be landed. During the drone's descent, the falcon is offered an easy meal having not made the criteria and, frustratingly, is positively reinforced for exhibiting an undesirable trait. One advantage of the drone is that the falcon always flies off the fist and remains ahead of you, given that the position of the drone is always upwind. Whereas, by contrast, the kite was always held in a downwind position, so the falcon flies behind you first. Typically, the pointer is upwind, so you ideally want the falcon to fly over the dog and really make the grouse clamp whilst making height. The drone excels in simplicity. I would no longer need Dobson to launch the kite; it would work in most average wind conditions, and I could nip out and fly Ballyhoo hard and return to The Box some 45 minutes later without much faffing.

As soon as I had mastered landing the parachute and falcon safely, I found that the speed and consistency of using the drone enabled not just greater accuracy, but also the ability to recognise and develop a falcon's flying style. I was fortunate that Stu had taught me the importance of striving to achieve a decent flying style the previous season. Stu's experience and knowing eye maximised the efficiency of each session. Ballyhoo was clipping and rowing without skipping a beat, ready for the tour.

When we arrived in the Cairngorms, the bothy felt very much home from home. With familiarity, we busied ourselves unpacking the vehicles and filling the fridge. The rear suspension of my truck audibly gasped as the crates of Guinness and a barrel of Wozale were offloaded. We were all delighted to learn Bishop had stowed his home-made pork pies and scotch eggs in the boot of his truck, rather than devouring them en route.

The impatient pointers were just as excited. Stu had brought Roo's mother, Cody, this year. Cody had recovered from having been spayed, was fitter than Sham, and no stranger to running on a moor to produce grouse, so she was the obvious choice. It was great to reunite her with Roo once more. We put the peregrines out to weather, and they needed no invitation to jump in their baths and recover from the long journey. As they bathed, we marvelled at each falcon's immaculate condition, shared stories of training and dared to foretell what might be on the moor. A crunching of gravel announced the arrival of a car. We looked to see a small hire car pull into the driveway. I turned to the chaps, unable to hide the grin on my face. "There's one more surprise this year."

The door opened and a slim, athletic man, handsome, with boyish good looks, rose from the driver's seat. Instantly recognisable, he was still smiling and had the same piercing blue eyes. Henry Worsley stepped out to join us. Despite the intervening 24 years, he was almost completely unchanged.

Be it fate, or more likely, an algorithm, I had managed to make contact with Henry's wife Joanna some months prior to our tour of the Highlands. Faster than the rabbits that had bolted from the warrens in my youth, I wrote to Henry at length and told him about all the things I had been up to since our time together in South Shropshire. I couldn't believe it when he replied. I was delighted, and the high esteem in which I held him only increased as I learned of what he had achieved in the two decades since we last saw each other.

Henry had served his time in The Regiment. His time residing in Shropshire and popping to the next-door county of Hereford was long in the past.

Since our time together ratching for rabbits, Henry had busied himself commanding the 2nd Battalion of the Royal Green Jackets, leading a six-month reconnaissance mission in Helmand Province. In 2007 he successfully traced the footsteps of Shackleton's 1907 *Nimrod* expedition across Antarctica, arriving exactly 100 years to the day at Shackleton's 'Farthest South' before marching on to the South Pole. Also, returning to Antarctica on the centenary expeditions of Captains Scott and Amundsen, he had led a team of six soldiers in a race along the original 1912 route to be first to the South Pole – some 900 miles unsupported. He became the only person to have completed the classic routes of Shackleton, Scott and Amundsen to the South Pole... to name a few of his misdemeanours.

Correspondence with Henry was addictive and always inspirational. He never failed to fill his letters with envious content and rousing tones of inspiring leadership and rhetoric that left me buoyed and hungry for his next letter. He always signed off his correspondence: *Onwards, Henry.*

Henry explained that he had just retired, having played out the final stages of his distinguished military career working from Washington, liaising between British and American Special Forces. He'd had a blissful, well-deserved holiday with Joanna in Greece and was revving up to complete a Herculean mission to be the first man ever to cross Antarctica unaided and unassisted. His mission, fuelled by his infatuation with Shackleton and a desire to raise money for the Endeavour Fund – a charity that aided wounded servicemen and women – would begin in October.

"So you might be free around the beginning of September?" I asked. I was wishing aloud. I never expected Henry to join us in the Highlands for our *Peregrines over Pointers* tour. Then came his response. "That would be heavenly. I'll stay with you for a few days then venture north for a stag." And so Henry stayed with us in the bothy, eager for adventure with hawk and hound in the Highlands. I was beside myself with excitement at the prospect of introducing him to the chaps. I had so many burning questions to ask my boyhood hero. As per our previous arrangement with the estate, we arrived on the Saturday and took the sporting rights from the Monday. This gave

Henry and I plenty of time to re-connect. He was as eager to discover what I had done since our days ratching for rabbits in Shropshire as the chaps and I were to cross-examine this most elite of military men, and hear of his escapades around the globe. *Henry, is it true that...? Henry, have you ever...? Henry, tell us about...* Henry patiently indulged our infantile questioning and delighted us with snippets from his SAS adventures in the 1990s. In the evenings, we'd make a roaring fire and sit fixated by his lectures, including powerpoint presentations, on both his and Shackleton's Antarctic feats. He had us all enthralled, and I was reduced to wonderment before my childhood hero. Henry listened intently to all aspects of our discussions on falconry and let slip that he was thinking about getting a hawk in his retirement.

Later that evening, the head stalker arrived and opened up more of the estate for us to explore. We had a bigger boundary to mark on the map and an extra three thousand acres to explore. One of the most important duties each evening was to keep a watchful eye on the weather forecast, especially the wind direction. From the forecasts, we'd carefully plot our approach, swooning over the maps as we studied the contours. Using metres above sea level to gauge heather length, and contours to gauge windward slopes, we aimed our approach towards favourable grouse locations.

In the morning, after a hearty breakfast, we loaded up the Land Rovers. Henry was adamant he'd lead the way and path-find towards the windward slopes that would give us an advantage. It would be about a 30-minute off-road drive from the bothy to where we needed to alight from the vehicles then ascend the hill. That morning the rain was quite heavy. There were glimmers of blue sky in the distance and the forecast was for a pleasant afternoon, so we set off in the drizzle, hoping it would dry up by the time we parked up. But it didn't. The drizzle got heavier and the blue sky we had spotted in the distance all but disappeared as the rain closed in. "I don't know how much you know about exploring, Henry, but in these conditions, us falconers do things a little differently," I said as I leaned over the bulkhead of the Land Rover and pulled the luncheon basket into the cab. Henry and I set about Bishop's home-made pork pie and Scotch eggs as the rain continued. It didn't look like the rain would be stopping anytime soon, so a bottle of port made an appearance, from which we supped a couple of glasses and continued to reminisce about our rabbiting skirmishes. "No, this is quite different to what I'm familiar with, though I could probably get used to it," Henry said.

Henry enjoys port and pie in the Land Rover, waiting for the rain to stop. ©Dave Warren

Eventually, the rain subsided and we got ourselves ready to climb the hill. The plan was to then roll over the top to the windward slope and hope to find grouse. We were all fit, kind of, but Henry's experience gave him a marked advantage and he set off blazing a trail to the locations he'd earmarked the night before. Behind him, we were charged by his energy and enthusiasm; his leadership prevented us from giving up and stopping to chance smaller bits of heather on the way. Instead, he pushed on towards the tops of the slopes. Needless to say, he was always first to the trig point and barely out of breath.

If we wanted to find the grouse, we'd have to discover the specific habitat regions, the 'Goldilocks zone' where the grouse tend to dwell. The maps told us of relevant geographical features but nothing of flora and fauna. We were walking into new regions without any knowledge of whether grouse would be there, and if they were, in what numbers.

We walked on and the ridgeline flattened. We kicked up a covey of four grouse, then in short succession an adult pair with three young. Henry had done his job and competently got us to the windward slopes among the grouse with the least exertion and disturbance. It was now time to run the pointers, mark a good set-up and put the falcons in a position to catch grouse. Stu peeped his whistle, which was the cue for Cody, his faithful pointer bitch, to drop to the ground and await being cast.

For some reason, both Ballyhoo and Gilbert had very mediocre flights, with nothing to show or remark upon. I was a little upset as nothing extraordinary or exhilarating was on show for Henry to marvel at. Both falcons were upstaged on this occasion by Bishop's falcon, Big Al. He was a tiny Barbary falcon weighing in at just 15 oz – about 7 oz smaller than the average male peregrine. Big Al had never been encouraged to chase prey and had only ever flown to a swung lure in flying demonstrations. Nevertheless, Bishop was looking after him and had brought him on tour so he could exercise and give this little falcon he was fond of a zoom-around after the important business had been concluded. For the last part of the day, Bishop decided he would not get the lure out and just let Big Al have a fly about. Big Al was so fixated on people that he would stay close to us, and we could simply walk back to the cars whilst he enjoyed whizzing around us for fun. After about five minutes of following us and not being presented with a lure, Big Al began to climb. To our astonishment, he made half a grand as we continued to walk back towards the trucks. Continuing his ascent, he was now at about 800 feet, just at the point where we accidentally disturbed some grouse not far from us. As soon as they had lifted, Big Al held a perfect stoop, tear dropping after them and *bloody nearly* connecting. I don't think he was big enough to have dealt a clinical blow, nor pin one to the ground, but regardless, Big Al had ideas above his station. It was an exciting spectacle, and had we disturbed snipe or plover, we could have been in for a well matched battle. "The trouble with Big Al is that no one has told him he's small," Bishop joked. Impressed by Al's efforts, Bishop was hungry to encourage this newfound behaviour and give him a flight or two at teal on the lowland.

All this walking up and down steep mountain ranges was thirsty work. When we returned to the bothy, Bishop and I remained steadfast that Guinness was the most appropriate drink to quench our thirst, but Stu was a seasoned tea drinker and Henry was in training. "Another tea, Henry?" Stu asked.

"No thank you, Stu, I've had my fill," came the reply. Whatever he lacked in fitness, Stu was delighted to discover that his new superpower was out-drinking the former SAS and British Army officer in cups of tea.

"The kettle don't stop in my house." Stu said with a smile as he walked outside with another brew and a freshly rolled cigarette.

Joining him outside in the evening sun, Henry lit a cigar and gleaned more information from Stu about grouse hawking. Stu needed no invitation to talk at length about his passion, and entertained Henry with his many stories. We all reflected on the tour – the greatest delight I took from which was developing Roo under Stu's guidance: watching in awe as she learnt her craft, naturally developing beautiful, flat, even patterns, being honest on every grouse pointed. The venue and sport far exceeded our worth. We had great flights and plenty of *bloody nearlies*, with the peregrines being outdone by the grouse.

On the final morning, we cleaned the bothy and headed into the village for a cooked breakfast. Henry was insistent that he should pay. We ate well, hugged and wished each other all the best. Henry smiled and said *fortitudine vincimus* (by endurance we conquer), got into his car and headed north. We turned south and headed for home, already looking forward to being back on the highlands next year.

Stu, Gilbert and Cody ©Leopold Amory

But Not To Yield

Plenty of phone calls ensued between Stu and me following the tour. We re-lived all the action; the stoops, the rakes, the splitters, the *bloody nearlies* and the sublime dog work. We spent November and December listening to Henry's podcast from Antarctica, making sure we both kept tabs on his Herculean efforts. When the phone rang in mid-december, I answered it with my usual delight at seeing Stu's name appear. I was anticipating another lively chat about Henry's progress or another chance to reminisce about the tour. Before I could finish my greeting, Stu shut me down. "Listen a minute, I need to get this out. You know I was a bit slow in eating the meals on holiday? Well, I had a lump in my throat and it was painful to swallow. Anyway, Mand's forced me for tests and... and it's an aggressive cancer. It's going to kill me. I've been given just over a year to live."

He paused and I listened to the familiar sound of him exhaling. "Dave, are you there?" Stu asked.

"Yeah, I heard you." I knew how to respond to his question, just not his revelation.

"There is a treatment option, it's..." but before Stu had finished his sentence I cut in:

"Well go for the fucking treatment."

"It's not that simple." Stu went on to explain that the radiotherapy and chemo had only a 50 per cent chance of working, was brutal and needed to start immediately. "If the treatment works, I'll be in remission, but if it doesn't work it will kill me sooner. I'll be dead in about four months' time – it will be torturous." Stu paused.

"You've got to go for the fucking treatment," I said. "Have a think please, Stu."

Stu hung up the phone. Over the next few days, he went through his options with Mandy and bravely opted for treatment. It had to commence quickly, so there was little time to complete the preparations, and within a fortnight, Stu found himself at the dentist having all 30 of his teeth pulled out in one sitting. A full-face mould was fabricated to hold his head and neck in position whilst he received radiotherapy. He shaved all his hair off and began his diet of liquified food and high-calorie milkshakes.

As a true falconer, Stu's overriding consideration was his peregrines. Without question, I caned my credit card into the red and purchased materials to quickly build falcon chambers in my garden that would house Gilbert and Ballyhoo. The option of selling-up never crossed our minds. Stu and I both knew that selling the game hawks would depress him so much that he wouldn't be able to muster the positivity or optimism needed to pull him through the treatment. With time against us, Stu drove himself to Scotland between bouts of treatment to hand over the falcons. He needed to see for himself that the birds were settled in, enabling him to focus on the battle ahead.

When Stu and I visited each other, we'd never knock on the door. It was a beautiful arrangement I've yet to experience with anyone else. Banging on the door sets the dogs off and chaos ensues. Our alternative was to simply walk in and find the kettle. If there wasn't anyone about, you'd make a brew and wait. If there was, you'd make two. On this occasion I hadn't realised Stu had arrived. I was returning from the garden and walked into the kitchen to find a figure standing next to the kettle. I didn't recognise him. Having started his treatment, he was now very gaunt. Without his wispy white locks of hair, and his teeth, his face had lost its structure. He was a shell of the man who, only a few months earlier, was striding up mountains. My heart sank as the gravity of the situation truly hit me. Stu could read my reaction instantly. He overly exaggerated his jaw movement to draw moisture from his throat, and it was as much as he could do to croak, "We'll leave the falcons on the cadge tonight."

I paused. I could see he had another sentence in him that he wanted to get out, so I waited patiently as he sipped his tea and built himself up to speaking again. "Now you have a go at saying that with no fucking teeth."

Stu finished the sentence with a smile and looked warm-heartedly at me; he hadn't lost his wit and was using his humour to console me. As he spoke in a muffled, slurred tone, I noticed his lips were cracked and bloody. His ever-kind eyes were a welcome distraction, and the only thing I could focus on as he wiped saliva from his chin.

The following morning, we put the finishing touches to the aviaries, garnished the perches with food and placed the falcons in their new home. "They'll have a clean moult and be ready for you next season," I promised as I locked the aviaries. I then turned to face Stu. He was smiling, but his eyes could not hide his sadness. Standing there in silence, we both welled up in knowing Stu might not be there when the aviary door re-opened.

A brew was the only outlet, so we headed inside for a cuppa. Roo was unapologetic about nuzzling into Stu. She recognised him and instantly picked up on the warmth and affection he showed her. Stu and I often spoke about the next generation of pointers. Having gifted Roo to me, the deal was that Stu would select the sire for her next litter and remain in control of his lifelong pointer progeny. I asked Stu to arrange this. "I want you to get better and I'll have a pup waiting for you on the other side," I told him. We needed optimism and positivity that would take him beyond the treatment. Roo would be in season come the middle of January, so a window of opportunity was opened with the owner of the chosen sire.

The next day, Stu and Mandy headed north for a quick lap of Scotland. For nostalgia's sake, he wanted to take Mandy on a tour of all the moors he had hawked on, spending time together in his favourite wilderness. The very next week, Stu was home and paying regular visits to Addenbrooke's Hospital to endure his harrowing cancer treatment. When Stu felt strong enough, we'd have brief phone calls. There was little to report back other than the news that his hawks were in rude health and safe in my aviary.

*****

Despite being (nearly literally) poles apart, Stu and Henry both spent Christmas Day fatigued, yet both still managed to make the most of it. Stu was bedridden, but strong enough to sit up, enjoy a cigarette and receive visits from his loved ones. Henry was about 100 miles from the South Pole on his solo expedition, tucked up in his sleeping bag, opening presents from family whilst supping a dram of 16-year-old Dewar's Royal Brackla. Henry was unable to see the far end of his tent through the smoke of one of his favourite Monte Cristo cigars. "Heaven", he described it.

Henry had travelled more than 800 miles unaided and unassisted across the most inhospitable environment on the planet; his body had endured severe hardship and virtually every part of him was in pain. Yet, in spite of being on the verge of collapse, he found inner strength to remain steadfast to his mission. *Always a little further*, a line from James Elroy Flecker's 1913 poem – and the SAS's unofficial motto – was painted on the front of Henry's sled. He drove onwards with the words of Tennyson's "Ulysses" in his head: *To strive, to seek, to find, and not to yield.*

Henry didn't yield. Forging through a whiteout on the 17th of January, he pulled his sled for 16 hours straight. He was struggling, and it took him until one o'clock in the morning to build camp, melt snow for cooking and transmit his update, the transmission fading in and out. *"It's now one o'clock in the morning, in sum, it's been a punishing day. So breathless . . . I am fading . . . hands/fingers are forever shutting down . . . wonder how long they will last."*

Seventy-one days into his 80-day mission, having covered a staggering 913 miles, Henry was just 30 miles short of achieving his objective when, like Shackleton, he *"shot his bolt"*. He was forced to end his adventure through sheer exhaustion, and at the request of his family. "My summit is just out of reach," he said. Shackleton's immortal words must have been ringing in Henry's ears as he was air-lifted off the ice. "A live donkey is better than a dead lion, isn't it?"

Having returned to Union Glacier base camp, Henry was being treated for dehydration and malnourishment. But it was quickly discovered that he was also suffering from bacterial peritonitis and was immediately flown to a hospital in Punta Arenas, Chile, for life-saving treatment. But despite the best efforts of the doctors, Henry's body was unable to respond and heal. On the 24th of January 2015, a hero died

I took an early flight from Scotland to arrive at St. Paul's Church in Knightsbridge, London, for Henry's funeral. I was just one of hundreds gathered, including the patron of the Endeavour Fund, Prince William. The eulogy recounted Henry's highly decorated career, his love for his family and his unwavering readiness to help those less fortunate. I smiled in great fondness when his love of ferrets was mentioned. Henry's son, Max, read a beautiful poem written for his father. The profoundly moving part of the service was the haunting reverberations of the Royal Green Jackets' lone bugler sounding 'The Last Post'. As Henry had once ushered my head down a rabbit hole so that I might first hear the sounds of a ferret bolting rabbits, I was now gripped in his presence, listening for the first time to the evocative cry of a sole bugle as the congregation said a final goodbye.

I sat, choked up and raw.

Henry Worsley ©Sebastian Copeland

Always A Little Further

"Dave it's Stu. We can go again." Stu had been for a check-up and the treatment had done its job. "The cancer's in remission. Although I'm mostly bedridden, I'm going to walk all 30 of Henry's untrodden miles and be fit enough for *Peregrines over Pointers*. I'm going to do it."

To this day, I have never felt so elated on hanging up a phone. The news had me punching the air and shouting in ecstasy, so-much-so that a heavily pregnant Roo left the comfort of her heat lamp and whelping crate to investigate the noise. A few nights later, on St Patrick's Day, Roo went on to have her litter of three bitches and four dogs. There was one puppy in particular who was a bold yet considered character. He never failed to catch my eye. I registered an affix with the Kennel Club, and named my new boy none other than 'Onwards Henry'.

Roo's litter, with Onwards Henry in the middle. 📷©Dave Warren

Stu chipped away at those untrodden miles each day throughout the spring in a bid to get fit enough to take to the moor in September. He was very weak and frail, but with dogged determination, Mandy holding his arm and Cody by his side, he shuffled round his local park and walked all Henry's lost miles. Bit by bit, his fitness was improving. "I'm as fit as I will ever be and should be good for the hill – mostly the down-hill," Stu proudly announced on the phone. He had managed to get himself into an eligible state, and naturally I was elated.

Though I didn't want to have to spoil the moment, I felt Stu would want to know of a predicament I was dealing with. At the risk of extinguishing the flames that fuelled Stu's recovery, I had to tell him. "I picked Ballyhoo off the floor of the aviary this morning. He's dead."

I was conflicted in my own emotions at losing Ballyhoo. It was a crying shame he was dead; however, feeling sorrowful felt very selfish given the magnitude of Stu's situation. I needed to put on a brave face, box in my loss and remain upbeat for the sake of his recovery. When I looked over Ballyhoo's body, there was nothing remarkable to indicate a cause of death. He hadn't exhibited any signs of ill health, and his body was trauma free. There in the evening, gone in the morning. A complete mystery and a terrible misfortune.

That afternoon, Stu was back on the phone. I think the loss of Ballyhoo caused him some anguish. Up until this point, Stu was only thinking about stumbling around on the moor next spring, but now he was perturbed; he felt he needed to plan ahead and future-proof our dream. Gilbert's parents were also, sadly, dead. It transpired that Gilbert was the only female peregrine bred by Hollidge from that line – the precious 'Holy Grail' some might say. Gilbert was sub-adult and there was a slim chance she might breed. Stu didn't need any reminding how precious life was and, recognising this lineage was on a knife edge, decided that the best option would be to keep Gilbert safe in the aviary and pair her with an older male. This would safeguard the line and keep us in peregrines for evermore. Gilbert was to stay in my aviary and be introduced to a handsome suitor.

Stu's decision was both rational and sensible. The ballpark price of female peregrine was creeping north of £4,000 in hard cash, an expense far out of reach of the likes of us working-class heroes. In contrast, male peregrines went from around £350 up to about £500. My falconry opportunities were certainly limited to flying males. Stu wanted to see me fly a young female, and this would be the only way he could foresee it happening, whilst also safeguarding the Hollidge line.

Attention turned to peregrine acquisition once more. Hollidge was not breeding, so we needed to look elsewhere for a couple of tiercels. The natural choice was to phone Professor Matt Gage, falconer, biologist and researcher. He possessed a nice line of peregrines, known in the industry as the Dixon line. They were not the largest of birds, but renowned because every falconer who flew the progeny of the ancestors of the Dixon line remarked on their natural willingness to wait-on, which is the *sine qua non* of a good gamehawk. Dobson and Gage were great friends as well as academic peers. They used to scoff at the idea that peregrines had been line-bred to achieve a better potential to wait-on, not least because they doubted that the animals had been through enough captive generations for the relevant genes – should they exist – to become fixed. Yet, in the last decade of his life, Gage became equally convinced that his own line of peregrines had done exactly that. He was at a loss to explain it any other way "… but mine just do," Gage said with a smile and a shrug.

If this phenomenon was to be true, a couple of clutch brothers would be perfect, and relatively easy for us to train. I telephoned Gage and asked if he had any available. He had only bred two males that season but sadly they were spoken for. It was his intention to fly one of them alongside a friend with whom he hawked grouse in Caithness. The phone call continued, and in learning of Stu's recovery and our predicament, Gage didn't deliberate: he selflessly told us to come and collect them. He and his friend would make other arrangements. Stu and I met at Gage's home in East Anglia, and to our delight, Gage's wife, Sylvie, had lovingly provided savouries for me and a wholesome fruit smoothie for Stu. We had lunch, laughed and were sent on our way with good will and sibling tiercels. Stu and I decided on a Shackleton theme for naming the brothers. I called mine Ernest and Stu decided on Mustard, after Colman's spicy donations to the Nimrod expedition.

Stu and I trained Ernest and Mustard throughout July and August, and got ourselves in good shape for September. Bishop collected Stu, and the pair drove over the border and met me at our Highland bothy. Against all odds, we were back on tour.

Stu was in great spirits. His body had slowed but his wit remained lightning fast. Still in recovery, Stu was mostly bedridden and tired quickly in the evenings. Keeping food and protein shakes down was impossible for him, and throwing them up was commonplace when he pushed his body too hard traversing the uplands. Remission wasn't easy. When hawking in the Highlands, you quickly learn that you need to keep moving. Remaining stationary and breathing out carbon dioxide without a midge net can be a fate worse than death. Bishop and I began to get midged as we waited for Stu to catch up. Stu only had one gear, and that was a very slow plod, cautiously placing his feet with each step. Midge attacks were a complete oversight on my behalf, and as we stood there in a cloud of them, I was suddenly very worried for him. Stu got a bit closer to us. "Can't complain too much, the fucking midgies won't touch me – must be the chemo!" He laughed, delighting in his new superpower.

Ernest and Mustard were great fun to fly. They just seemed to go up, wait on, and come down. This gave us the opportunity to relax, as with each flight, we grew in confidence that they were settling into a consistent and reliable routine. They both learned the game and the *bloody nearlies* increased. Against the spirit of the meet, Bishop snuck his gyr-peregrine hybrid onto the card, A faux-pas that was met with merciless ribbing. Jesting aside, Bishop was plagued with rotten luck on each flight, mostly the grouse breaking early, which made his attempts to instil waiting-on all the more challenging. Through no fault of his own, the grouse would flush early, and his falcon would naturally rocket in hot pursuit of the fleeing grouse, with very low odds of success. This turned him into a bit of a pursuit hawk. Such untimely rewards served to demonstrate how, without progressive training and consistent timely jackpotting, a young falcon's mindset cannot be moulded.

In spite of having little appetite, and the loud protests of his body, each evening Stu would mash up mince and tatties and force himself to swallow all he could in order to keep going. His strawberry meal shakes were 500 calories, and he would aim for three-a-day. These and mushed cottage pie were his sole foodstuffs. Anything else, he said, tasted too metallic or salty. Stu would head up to bed early each night, leaving Bishop and me to wash up and close the house down.

The evenings were quite sober affairs for Bishop and me. With Stu in remission and exhausted, there wasn't much banter to be had. The front room that was once full of bravado and adventure stories was quiet. Bishop and I stitched hoods, and the only sound to break the silence was the occasional quiet hiss of a can of Guinness.

We finished the tour, and Bishop and Stu drove back to East Anglia. Packing up the bothy felt quite normal, Stu was in reasonable fettle and on the mend. The pair continued to hawk on the lowlands of East Anglia. The stubble fens proved easier than the mountainous rank heather, and Stu's health, albeit poor, was good enough to get flights on the partridges. His friends Steve Moore, Bishop and Hollidge would generously invite him onto their beats. They kept his tail wagging.

In a cruel twist of fate, optimism turned to tragedy. Stu's regular check-in with his oncologist brought devastating news, which kicked the legs from beneath him. A newly found shadow revealed that his lungs were pebble-dashed with incurable, aggressive cancer nodes that gave him a life expectancy of about 12 months. Stu phoned me and relayed the news. Our hearts sank as the glimmer of hope we clung to was snatched away unforgivingly and indefinitely.

"But until I sicken, I'm not going to give in to it." Stu was resolute. Remarkably, Stu felt well enough. He had little body fat, his muscles were repairing and he was a lot more active having returned from the Highlands. Stu flew Mustard into the new year and had one of his best-ever seasons flying the plucky tiercel. At the end of the season, Stu put Mustard in his aviary to moult. He was adamant that he would reclaim him from the aviary in five months' time, and we'd go again.

As ever, with the falcons moulting feathers in the safety of the aviaries, attention turned to the dogs. I had two very athletic prey-driven pointers to consider. Roo needed to maintain a good level of fitness, and Henry was just about ready to be introduced to the moor and needed some gentle training. I spent a good period of the springtime running them on the moor and counting grouse. The plan was also to use this opportunity to train them so that fewer mistakes were made under the falcon.

Since Henry's funeral, I had stayed in touch with Henry's son, Max. In our correspondence, I shared tales about his father and our adventures in the Highlands. I kept him up to date with the progress of Onwards Henry and, intrigued, Max accepted my invitation to join me in Scotland, to work the pointers and venture into the Cairngorms. I had wanted to ask Max something on the run-up to his arrival, but I worried that it might come across as morbid or insensitive. In the end, I plucked up the nerve to ask him if he had any of the sled ropes from his father's Antarctic expedition. For sentimentality and a keepsake, I wanted to fashion a dog lead for Onwards Henry that would keep Henry's memory alive, and inspire a bit of fortitude in the field. "He would have loved the idea of that," Max replied. On his arrival he gifted to me a couple of lengths of rope that Henry had used to pull his sled on his fateful mission. We had a beer (or two), chatted into the evening, and I stitched the rope into a lead for Onwards Henry.

*****

Roo was a very methodical and steady bitch. She could be trusted to work between young broods of grouse without fear of chomping them. As such, I was granted permission to run her on my friend's moor and provide detailed grouse counts on some areas of heather regeneration. From my figures, if grouse were in good numbers with a favourable ratio of young to old, the keeper would know whether it was worth making these areas part of a shoot. My reward was a chance to give Henry a run and begin his career.

I woke Roo and Henry up and loaded them into the truck at 3 am. It took about one and a half hours to reach the beat and I arrived around 4:30 am as the sun was beginning to make its way up. I took Roo out and she ran in lovely fashion. I was able to keep a straight beat and gain a good idea of the breeding success in a patch of regeneration heather. It was about 6 am. I was alone on a big moor and it was time to set Onwards Henry off for his first lesson and embark on my first time training a pointer without Stu's company. His voice reverberated in my head. *Keep the brakes on him* and *don't let the elastic snap.*

The breeze had picked up a little, so keeping him running in quartering fashion was made slightly easier. I kept his beats purposely short so he would not lose sight of the whistle. Henry proved very biddable and turned each time of asking. This made his quartering very even. By talking and encouraging him on each pass I let him know he was running beautifully; I just hoped he'd hit the scent of grouse rather than bump into a hare. Luckily, he did, and held the point well. As we moved in, the adult grouse lifted. I was close enough to Henry to command him to drop and wait. I gave him gentle praise to let him know he was doing well, then, with a click of my fingers, he moved onwards and froze once more. We continued in this fashion, and he produced five grouse in turn, under full control. He was a natural. Having cleared the immediate area, I flung the lead around his neck and praised him heavily for his efforts. His training progressed; mistakes were few and far between and he was allowed to range further and further. The more he ran, the more he understood. Capturing his natural ability was relatively easy, just that stroke down the back of his neck and gentle communication was enough. Henry was a very soft, delicate pointer around his birds – but when in search of them, he was a steam train.

I had Henry running to such a fine standard that I thought I'd chance my arm and see where he measured against the country's finest, so I entered him into his first field trial.

*****

Pointers and Setters have formally competed against each other since 1865, when the first ever field trials were established. Their style, grace, game-finding ability and obedience were pitted not only against their closest breeds – English setters, Irish setters and Gordon setters – but within the pointer breed itself. Classes were separated by ability (puppy, novice and open stake), rather than sex or age (save for pups under two years). This competition of dogs proved to provide a benchmark against which the continuation of the breed would be measured. The popularity of shooting, particularly red grouse, opened the doors for huge kennels to establish. The two World Wars dealt punishing and devastating blows to the industry and breed. Heartbreakingly, thousands of pointers, setters and working dogs of every ilk were destroyed. There was simply no-one to look after them and no food to feed them. The kennel hands and masters went to war, many were shot and killed, but some survived, and the dogs that had been placed in the care of their wives and families were the foundation for many of today's lineages and were used to resurrect the breed.

Field trials resumed from 1946, but the prevalence of the pointer in the field and on the moor subsequently has never reached the level of the pre-war era.

There are three stakes in the field trial: the Puppy, the Novice and the Open Stake. The field trial winner is placed first in the Open Stake. Only when a dog wins two Open Stakes are they awarded Field Trial Champion status.

*****

Henry was only eligible to be entered into the Puppy Stake, but if he won, he would qualify to run in the Open Stake, bypassing the Novice standard. I got up early and travelled to Cawdor for Henry's first trial. The estate, and the majority of northern Scotland, was experiencing a low ebb in the natural cycle of grouse. This excited me as Henry had unreal pace and endurance. It was remarkable how good he was at covering the ground and I knew his running style would impress. In order to win any stake, the winning dog must produce a grouse for the gun and be shot over. If the grouse were few and far between, then hopefully Henry would maintain a good rhythm without distraction until he found the grouse.

In the Puppy Stake there was a mix of dogs and bitches including English setters, pointers and Irish setters. The draw for the Stake was made and I learned that Henry was in the first round against a pointer bitch with a great pedigree. Her sire and dam were both FT Champs and her handler was the very well respected, famed and capable handler, Richard MacNicol. Dreams of being drawn against a comparatively slow-plodding Gordon setter in the first round were truly smashed.

We set our pointers down and cast them in opposite directions. I looked across at the bitch and saw she was rapid, too. Both pointers ran their first cast evenly, turned, crossed and headed out to the opposite flank. By their second turn, all was to play for. The two pointers were pretty evenly matched and I was pleased that Henry continued, undistracted. The pair crossed and the bitch turned early, as is sometimes the way with puppies, and she began to follow Henry. This must have spurred his competitive nature and he forged ahead with her in pursuit. MacNicol managed to turn his bitch to keep the brace separate and running in opposite directions, as is desirable, but by this time Henry was at the end of his beat and naturally turned himself. Ahead of him now was the bitch, running away from him. Henry tore after her in a full sprint, covering the ground with real venom and easily gaining on her. I could tell he was more in chase mode than hunting mode so, at the risk of him missing out on some ground where the bitch was about to pass, I turned him slightly early to give him the lead in the next cast. Fortune favoured me. Henry ran ahead of the bitch and was now the lead dog. He got onto the scent of grouse and locked solid on point. The bitch stopped too. She was exhibiting her class by backing and acknowledged the point. Regardless, Henry was the lead dog, and I claimed the point. MacNicol then stood by the bitch, keeping her still and preventing her from spoiling the flush. I levelled with Henry and, at the judges' request, clicked my fingers and commanded Henry into flush. An adult pair lifted, and Henry dropped as the shot was fired. Henry was unmoved. He was then required to clear out the expectant covey, but the pair were barren. We had done enough and were instructed to put the leads back on our dogs.

Of the nine puppies entered, four were invited back for the second round. Again, Henry made up a brace with another pointer. Having been shot over, Henry had done all that was required of him and just needed to stay honest, undistracted and not make any mistakes. He remained focused for the second round and ran a good pattern for five or six beats. The judges didn't run the pointers on for a lengthy spell and asked us to recall the dogs.

Henry had run in good form and took the opportunity in front of him with great style and obedience. He was awarded first place in the Puppy Stake – the Ruggles-Brise Trophy – and a small amount of cash, which I donated to The Endeavour Fund. I was made up and phoned Stu. He told me he could not have been more proud and delighted. It was the optimism Stu needed. He'd be excited to see Henry in September and get a flight over him. "Keep them both fit, don't let their pads go soft, we'll need 'em," Stu cautioned.

Winning the Puppy Stake ©Dave Warren

The Death Tour

Those five months took their toll on Stu. The grip and unforgiving onset of terminal lung cancer meant that his body was unable to repair itself, and was beginning to shut down. Stu was doing his best to pile food in, but an inability to properly digest his meals meant his body was now in a negative energy state. His mind remained as sharp as a tack and darkly humorous. The one and only thing he was deadly serious about was going grouse hawking in September.

Stu's bloody-mindedness somehow kept him going, and he decided to title Peregrines over Pointers 2017, 'The Death Tour'. It was Stu's wish for one of his most cherished friends, Helen Macdonald, to join us on the tour and share in his last hurrah. Helen was mentored by Stu during the training of her goshawk, Mable. Helen's mentorship began a few years prior to mine, but similarly fused the closest of bonds with Stu, Mandy and their family. Until this moment I'd only met Helen briefly over a bite to eat in Stu's kitchen. This would be the first occasion I would spend some time with her after having read her book and I eagerly anticipated the roar of Stu's V8 Discovery approaching my cottage. Admittedly, I was reduced to a fanboying state when they arrived – really quite nervous. After all, you never get a second chance at a first impression and I was anxious to provide a warm welcome. I was longing to give Mandy a huge hug and enjoy her trademark banter. Cody the dog was inbound and there would be some doggy delirium when she was reunited with Roo. Most importantly, Stu would need to sit down in the alpha chair, and a cup of tea would need to be readied. At least, these were my thoughts and intentions. Poor Helen was floored with a rotten migraine and sat suffering, eyes closed, in the passenger seat of the Discovery. Stu had determinedly driven all the way and, having spent six and a half hours in the saddle, was beginning to fatigue. Instead of sitting down to drink tea, his eagerness to cast an eye on his peregrines residing in my aviaries took priority. As such, it transpired that my cottage served as little more than a quick pit-stop as we elected, rightly, to get up the road. Standing on ceremony at the cottage was needless when the bothy was a few hours further north up the A9.

As we all began to settle in the bothy, it became apparent why Stu adored the manuscript he had proudly showed to me on the very first night of meeting him. It was a tangible extension of the immeasurably close friendship that Helen, Stu and Mandy shared. It was humbling to see their bond. Helen was patient and loving, and she radiated a kindness that mirrored Stu's and Mandy's affections for her. One consequence of Helen's loving nature was that it made her the target of a forthright Cody – dogs sense these things – and Cody's nose-nuzzling was unavoidable and impossible to reject. In between trips to the moor, we'd sit feeding falcons, relaxing, serving up parameter-hitting conversation, laugh and drink copious amounts of tea – enough to wash down the huge wedges of lemon drizzle cake that Stu forgave us eating in front of him. My very best attempts at completing the daily crosswords would result in frustration and little progress. Helen would put down the book she was reviewing, swoop in, finish the puzzle, and leave me feeling very much in awe of her black-belt literary genius.

Stu's mental resolve overshadowed his physical weakness in his quest for one final tour on the grouse. Knowing it was his last, he was unyielding. Each morning there was an opportunity to fly, he strapped into his gaiters and boots – though he was now so gaunt and light he was unrecognisable from the wild-haired, beaming giant that I'd first seen walking the moor. Once he was locked into his footwear, Stu remarkably managed to romp through patches of rank heather, even up and over peat hags.

Stu, unyielding. 📷©Leopold Armory

There was no greater time for our pointers to exhibit their class and ability. Life for Stu was literally too short to forgo missed opportunities. Should the grouse lift in the event of the dog failing to run a pattern, it would result in another hundred yards of energy- sapping marching through long heather, searching for another point. Should the dog put too much pressure on the grouse, causing it to flush when the falcon was out of position, the flight would be ruined. A false, unproductive point might offer up a follow-on opportunity for the falcon who was patiently waiting on, but might have taken Stu dangerously far from the safety of the track.

In our favour, we had three generations of Stu's pointers on the hill with us: Cody, Roo and Henry. Roo was set to do the lion's share. Stu noted that Roo was the best pointer he's ever produced and she gave him the most confidence to fly over. Cody was reliable, but now getting old, and her ground coverage was much reduced. Henry was fit and driven enough to take in the whole of Aberdeenshire, but he was still young and needed to learn his craft. He needed to learn to cope with the distraction of peregrines flying overhead. Stu's mentoring became extremely precious. I worked the dogs as best I could, knowing I only had a handful of opportunities left to draw from Stu's experiences in the field – a few last chances for him to observe, judge, critique and influence my handling of Roo and Henry.

Stu's gums bled each day. It was a self-inflicted trauma caused by striking the falcons' hood braces with his mouth. He had no other way of striking the braces to remove the hood. It didn't matter to Stu; he didn't care about the inconvenience. His overriding consideration, as ever, was managing Mustard's wellbeing and going hawking. In the evenings I'd wait for everyone to retire to bed and do the final check of the falcons and return their hoods to the sideboard. I remember, on one occasion, Stu had placed Mustard's hood on a small coffee table next to his chosen armchair. The hood braces were stained red and there was a fresh clotted string of blood that stretched between the hood brace and the coaster on which it was placed – it was the exact shape of an hourglass.

*****

The weather was inclement and provided only a handful of opportunities to get out on the hill. We got ourselves into some brilliant locations where both dogs and falcons repeatedly put on a spectacle. Mustard exhibited the most impressive flying between the sibling tiercels. Turning over at well over a grand, he had some very high stoops, but unfortunately he didn't manage to get his grouse. Once again, the plucky birds proved why they are the toughest quarry to pursue.

Ernest had one remarkable flight over Henry. I had walked on a little further downhill from the others, working Henry, when he went on point. I turned around to see that Stu, Mands and Helen were standing watching from about 100 metres up the bank. I unhooded Ernest and he made short work of getting to a grand whilst I moved round to advance the point. On my command, Henry flushed his grouse. There was one that split from the covey that flew up the banking towards the others. Ernest singled it out and raked it with such a crump that Stu, Helen and Mands emitted an audible *Oooh*, in awe of the hard impact. I put Henry back on his lead and together we made our way over to Ernest, who was plucking and scoffing his prize. It was the first grouse Henry had produced for the falcon, and he did it in fine style. Stu, Helen and Mands duly congratulated us, and we headed back to Peregrine Rock for photographs.

On the final day of the Death Tour, we had to put in a lot of dog work for only a couple of finds, yet this was enough to secure another couple of great flights and two exciting *bloody nearlies* for the peregrines. After finishing, we began a slow saunter back to the vehicles over some ground that had never produced grouse for us before. I looked back to the sound of Stu's whistle. He had quietly taken himself aside and set Cody down for what he knew would be their last cast together and his last ever handling of a pointer on the moor. He lifted the lead from Cody's neck, and she was cast off. After a few beats, Cody locked solid on point. Cody held firm and Stu slowly made his way down to her. As he levelled with her side, he clicked his fingers. Cody went on and produced a pair of grouse and froze once more. Stu once again levelled with her and clicked. Cody and Stu then systematically and delicately worked out the rest of the covey, flushing the remaining three in sequence and in exemplary form. Stu replaced the lead on Cody.

After remaining stoic and resolute all day, he was finally unable to contain himself and stood crying and inconsolable. Both Mandy and Helen rushed in and held him on his feet as he broke down. With two dogs held on leads on my right arm and a falcon on my left it would have been a calamity had I also run in. As such, I was forced to remain on the periphery and watch. The moment remained between them. It didn't seem real, but it was over. This would be Stu's last time on the moor and the last time he would work his pointers. I swallowed my tears and loaded my truck.

Cody, one final point. ✎©Amelia Siddle

Don't Count Your Chickens

Christmas and the New Year came and went, and it wasn't until we got into 2018 before Stu really began to make arrangements for after his death. He was beginning to get his house in order. Until that point, he had made no decisions about his beloved falcons. But on the phone one day he said, "I'm still not quite done in. We can go on one last breeding season to keep the dream alive. If nothing comes by the May bank holiday, quickly sell the pair. It's my funeral fund. I'm not letting Mands pay for that."

Stu wasn't cash or asset rich. The sale of his pair of peregrines for £5k would go a long way to covering his funeral expenses, a burden Stu was not prepared to pass to his surviving family. I spent many nights awake, deeply anguished in deciding if it was at all feasible for me to purchase Gilbert. £5k was well beyond my financial reach and I certainly didn't want Stu's charity. Paying back a £5k loan would wipe away any ready money I would need for getting by in the foreseeable future – I don't think my famously frugal grandmother would have approved! I asked myself, "would £5k be a more palatable, safer purchase if I wrapped Gilbert in cotton wool and she never leaves the safety of a breeding chamber?" But morally, was I prepared to prevent Gilbert a chance of climbing to the clouds and stooping ever again? I had so many ethical considerations to battle with. Gilbert might not breed for another three years, if at all. I couldn't leave her staring at four walls of an aviary for the rest of her long life, could I? I knew that after each unsuccessful breeding season, my intentions would be to send her into the wilderness on every possible occasion. In doing so, I'd subject her to the risks of predation, line collision, electrocution, getting lost, starvation, injury and other associated flying hazards. Could I do that on a whim, with £5k of my own money? I had done exactly this with Snatch at the Safari Park, but that wasn't my own money flying around, and it wasn't as much. I had been circumspect then, but who's to say being circumspect was in the best interests of Gilbert? Should the life of a peregrine be high octane and potentially cut short, or one of low exposure and increased longevity? Buying Gilbert would make financial sense if I treated her as an investment. If she was successful, I'd never have to buy another falcon.

Heavily torn, I concluded that buying Gilbert was, devastatingly, beyond me. I understood Stu's predicament and wanted to help as best I could, so I organised the sale. Gilbert was in my aviary, and the last thing Stu or Mandy needed was dealing with idiots on the phone or reclaiming her from the aviary then hand her to a stranger.

The falcons were just one of Stu's possessions that he knew Mandy had no desire to keep after his passing. Being the wife of a falconer was torment enough without having to shoulder the responsibility of the falcons as a widow. Stu set about getting rid of all the things Mandy wouldn't care for, mostly falconry-related kit, including his book collection and tracking devices, banking the money ready for his funeral package. He also got rid of his beloved motorbike, on which he and Mandy had zoomed round the southern counties and enjoyed trips to the coast most weekends.

Stu allowing the peregrines to stay with me for another breeding season in a bid to keep the dream alive was an insanely generous gamble. The falcons were in great health, in very good order and ready to sell. The sensible decision would have been to immediately cash them in. Prolonging their sale ran the risk of disease or escape and negated any chance of putting £5k in the undertaker's hand. There was also every chance that Stu himself might pass before his May bank holiday deadline. If any chicks came from this gamble, their rearing and branching would be well beyond Stu's life expectancy. Monies would be tied up and unavailable for the funeral until they had flown the nest. Nevertheless, the bell hadn't tolled, and Stu was still in control and determined to oversee the continuation of the 'Peregrines over Pointers' legacy. This might just be the way to do it.

As he weakened, telephone conversations between me and Stu became fewer and, naturally, shorter . But something happened in mid-April that made me desperate to speak to him. "Stu can't talk now Dave,' Mandy said on answering his phone. "I'm with him but he's very tired, in bed. He's had a bad couple of days.".

"Just whisper to him that Gilbert's laid her first egg!" I said. The line was quiet for a moment.

"*Oh my Christ!* He's just gone and put both thumbs up, that's the most he's managed all day," Manders exclaimed.

Gilbert completed laying a clutch of four eggs. She took turns with the tiercel and incubated them. I sent exciting updates to Stu and Manders. But on day 22 of the typical 29-day incubation period, Gilbert rejected all the eggs and kicked them off the nest ledge. Somehow, she knew they were all infertile. *La Tristesse Durera.*

*****

Put The Kettle On

I didn't want to sell Stu's falcons to an unvetted home, so in the hope she might take them, I spoke with one of my closest friends, Louise, a falconer and a successful breeder of peregrines. Unfortunately, her aviaries were full, and she had no accommodation to house the pair. She did, however, have a very close friend, Clive, who she knew would be interested. Louise couldn't speak highly enough of Clive. He was a trusted friend of hers, a salt-of-the-earth type with some lovely accommodation available. I'd known Louise for years. She's classic Yorkshire, forthright, calls a spade a spade – and although I didn't know Clive, if Lou vouched for him, he was good enough for me.

When Stu's health deteriorated further, his oncologist, Manders and the care team came to the inevitable conclusion that it was best for him to move to Arthur Rank Hospice, Cambridge. Stu still had Mustard in his home aviary, and it was his wish that I give him one more chance at a grouse before selling him for Mandy. Stu was meticulous in observing the falcons as they moulted their feathers. Prying through the carefully drilled 10 mm spy holes gave him the ability to hold off reclaiming them until they were ready, and never before. This time it was different. It was Mandy who decided it was time for me to come, see Stu and collect Mustard.

I knew this trip was going to be hard, and I forced myself to remain mechanical during the long drive down. I pulled up the driveway in the early evening, then, as ever, went through the front door to find the kettle. Stu was sitting on the sofa in his pyjamas and fondly greeted me with his warm piercing eyes and a wry gummy smile. We stayed up as late into the night as he could manage, laughing, drinking tea and reminiscing together as a light haze of Golden Virginia swirled around the kitchen. Normality was shattered when I handed Stu the envelope of cash from the sale of Gilbert. Stu took it and paused, contemplating the significance of what he was holding. He then turned to me and said, "Promise me you'll catch a grouse with him – Mustard deserves his grouse."

It was my turn to pause. The next time I walked out onto the moor, the next time Mustard took to the air, it would be without Stu. Again, as was often the case, Stu was first to break the silence, and spoke through red, water-shot eyes and a dry throat. "I don't want to leave you behind," Stu said, barely managing to get his words out. He hid his tears with a scrunched tissue and was almost fitting as the uncontrollable sobbing rocked his body. It was hard for me to watch him as he tried to speak. Stu and I never had a gushing relationship. We didn't show emotional vulnerability. Instead, we'd laugh and make light of each other's tribulations – after all, there was always the next day to put things right. As we sat there, lost in our muted state, I too had to acknowledge that this was the end. At first I thought it – *I may not get another chance to do this* – and then with dread, I said it.

"Tomorrow, Stu, I'm going to have to say goodbye to you."

We sat there, staring at each other. It was emotionally tortuous. We both knew this marked the end of our journey together. With an unspoken understanding, I stood up, gave Stu a hug and took myself upstairs to bed.

*****

"You got that fucking kettle on yet?" These were the first words I heard in the morning. It was Stu. He was taking his time as he carefully descended the staircase. One of Stu's most endearing qualities was his opening gambits. These were served to make you laugh and put you at ease. With this one line, Stu had made everything perfectly normal again, despite the pained effort it took for him to speak. His humour got us back into our usual routine. More importantly, it set the tone for the rest of the day – let's not ruin our last day together with emotional, physically draining breakdowns.

As usual, the kettle didn't stop, but sadly neither did the clock. As it neared 11am, I nipped into the aviary and got Mustard back on the block. It didn't take long before Mustard's posture went from thinned, withdrawn and relatively motionless, to fluffed up, confident and in a slightly animated state. He began to preen, bite at the jess, scratch at the hood and row up.

"You'd better get him under the tap, he's lively," Stu said forthrightly. Although largely incapacitated, he never lost his ability to control a situation. I left Stu in the kitchen and went outside to dampen Mustard's flight feathers under the hose. Once Mustard's feathers were soaked, I walked round the side of the house to delicately place him on the cadge in the boot of my truck. Mustard's wings were heavy and held low. He was unlikely to thrash around and damage them before I got on the road, so I closed the tailgate and turned around. Unbeknown to me, I was being watched. Stu had crept down the driveway. Placing Stu's falcon into my truck was my last act under the watchful eye of my mentor.

"That's it. You've graduated, I can't teach you anymore," Stu said over my shoulder and thrust his hawking vest at me. I held Stu in my arms as we both sobbed uncontrollably. He was a thin rag doll. If I had held him any tighter, I would have crushed him. "Will you speak at my funeral? Tell them, tell them what I was like – please, tell them what I was like."

As I held him, I replied "I will tell them, and I will never forget you. Every time I strike the hood braces, every time I cast the pointer, whenever the falcon takes to the wing – you'll be alive in me. Thank you, Stu, for everything. Love you fella."

We had reached the end of our run, our dream. The wet, reclaimed falcon on the cadge became the excuse not to prolong things. I don't know how my legs functioned, but I got into my truck and drove out of Whittlesford. Our time together was over.

One week later, Stu made his last journey out of the village. He held the head of his pointer, Cody, stared into her eyes, kissed her and thanked her for her love and service. Then, on finishing his cup of tea, he climbed into a wheelchair and was wheeled down the driveway to the hospice, leaving all he knew behind him forever.

Stu resided in The Arthur Rank Hospice until he passed on the evening of the 13th of August 2018. That night, he insisted his bed was wheeled outside so that he could feel the cool breeze and listen to birdsong. He was with his family, who were holding his hands and gently talking to him as he slipped away.

******

One final journey to Cambridge was required of me. Before setting off from Scotland, I collected the brightest-flowering ling and bell heather in order to connect Stu with the moor one last time. The heather formed a wreath around the block perch on which Mustard presided. Mustard was immaculately turned out and wearing one of my best grouse-plume hoods. Stu arrived at the crematorium in a Harley Davidson hearse. It was to be the last motorbike ride he and Mandy took together. They were flanked by about 50 of his biker pals. It was quite the procession that thundered into the car park. Before heading inside, I chatted with Stu's son, Sam, Mandy and Helen. Mustard received much attention; he was looking smart in a painted and plumed grouse hood. Mandy then asked if I remembered the first decent plumed hood I'd made for Stu. Of course I did. "Well, he's still got it, he wanted it in his casket with him."

The crematorium was packed with friends and family. Cody was dressed in a Guns N' Roses bandanna. She sat in the front row and Mustard was placed on Stu's casket for the entirety of the funeral service.

Fulfilling the promise I'd made to him, I spoke at the funeral and told those gathered what Stu was like. I told them how he often described himself as a working-class hero, that he was never greedy or materialistic, and was generous to a fault. More honourably, he was a humble gentleman, and always stayed true to his word.

Stu often said to me, "I've got nothing, but I'll give you half of nothing." On one of our last times together, he gave me his tweed suit and instructed me to wear it to his funeral. True to his word, on the day, only half of it fitted. Although he said he had nothing, when measured against the old idiom, "*If you want to find out how rich you are, you count the things you have that money can't buy*" his wealth was vast. And it survives so generously in his influence and in all the fabulous memories I will cherish.

Helen then read a beautiful and fitting tribute to Stu and ended by reciting a poem by John Gillespie Magee, an Anglo-American aviator and poet. Magee served in the Royal Canadian Air Force. Although his verse was written in the 1930s, his words touched us all in a final fitting tribute to our friend.

> Oh! I have slipped the surly bonds of Earth
> And danced the skies on laughter-silvered wings;
> Sunward I've climbed, and joined the tumbling mirth
> of sun-split clouds, — and done a hundred things
> You have not dreamed of — wheeled and soared and swung
> High in the sunlit silence. Hov'ring there,
> I've chased the shouting wind along, and flung
> My eager craft through footless halls of air...
>
> Up, up the long, delirious, burning blue
> I've topped the wind-swept heights with easy grace.
> Where never lark, or even eagle flew —
> And, while with silent, lifting mind I've trod
> The high untrespassed sanctity of space,
> – Put out my hand, and touched the face of God.

At the end of the funeral we headed to a nearby pub for refreshments. Everyone had just about stopped crying and was in need of a drink. Stu's son, Sam, was standing at the bar. "Is it Guinness you're after?" I asked, keen to buy him a pint. But Sam had another idea.

"No, I'm being served, thanks. In memory of my old man, I'm waiting for a nice cup of tea."

*****

PART 3:

ONWARDS

We shall not cease from exploration
And the end of all our exploring
Will be to arrive where we started
And know the place for the first time.

–T.S. Eliot

Flying Solo

Despite concerted efforts at indoctrination by the Church of England during my primary school education, as well as my fond memories of Reverend Payne, and growing up next to a graveyard, I am not religious. That said, I am also not such a staunch atheist to eliminate the slim possibility of an alternative realm. Amidst all my scepticism, I do find *huge* comfort in simply accepting the unknown – ignorant bliss. Maybe there are things that we simply do not have the ability to fathom. Maybe there are undescribed or unknown realms where our soul (let's call it that) transitions once the body is spent. I appreciate it certainly can't be argued as fact, nor even likely – but there's no reason to deny myself some wonderment, or a version of events to hope for after we exhale our last.

What we hope for, we look to reaffirm. Coincidental happenings, especially natural phenomena, bring comfort and cast colour on our outlook while thinking of the long or recently dead. In my case, it was a timely rainbow saturating a dull moorland with vibrancy whilst I reflected on Stu. For Henry Worsley, it was thoughts of Shackleton when the sun, ice, and air combined to create a glowing halo over Antarctica.

I paid witness, as my old friend Mike did with his mother, to Stu slowly ebbing away. Firstly, he had all his teeth extracted, then endured barbaric, brutal chemo and radiation treatment in an attempt to rid his body of cancer. Next, he bravely coped with pain and the heavy onset of a cancer that would see him unable to control his balance, unable to consume anything other than mashed food and protein shakes, unable to hold down fluids, suffering daily from a parched mouth, uncontrolled bleeding of the gums and extreme fatigue. Then, ultimately, he was made to watch all that he loved move beyond his grasp. The cancer, however, was powerless to kill his mental resolve and ambition to keep casting his peregrine into the wind. His head and heart drove him to the moor. And it was on the moor that Stu walked tall, with purpose and conviction, masking his pain, hunger and thirst. On the moor, he experienced weightlessness whilst watching his pointer quarter the heather in front of him and his peregrine flitting through the clouds above him. Here was his heaven.

Venturing to the Highlands within four weeks of Stu's funeral for another 'Peregrines over Pointers' tour was incredibly hard. The sorrow I felt in driving the tracks and walking in Stu's footprints weighed heavy on me, and being there without him felt wrong. The flames that once raged within me to practise falconry were now as pathetic as the green oak fires I tried to light in The Box. It was the lowest I'd ever felt with a hawk on my fist. The only motivation that prevented me from turning home was what Stu had made me promise: *"Take him and catch a grouse with him."*

With Mustard and Ernest on the cadge, I roamed the Cairngorm mountain range with a raw throat and heavy legs. What I knew to be an exhilarating highland adventure was now simply a matter of fact. I felt like I was just going through the motions and didn't really know where I wanted to be. I was lost within our familiar landscape. Stu's absence made no impact on Roo or Henry; they were overcome by prey drive and the innate impulse to run. The leads that had once dragged Henry's sled were now dragging me across the heather as the pointers leaned into the moor. Similarly, Mustard had a new servant of convenience, and desired to blaze updrafts and stoop. He was rousing lots and biting at the glove in a state of heightened readiness.

Onwards Henry 📷©Dave Warren

As my boots scuffed through the heather, I could sense that everything else was suddenly still and quiet. I looked up, unaware that Henry was locked solid on point, halting the natural ebb and flow of his beat. I stopped and watched him. Henry remained solid on point, then lay down flat on his belly. He did this when he felt he was within touching distance of a clamped grouse. It was warm and mid-afternoon. Scenting conditions were poor, and even the best long-nosed dog would struggle hunting grouse at distance today. But he was right on it.

Trust your dog. I could hear Stu's voice reverberating round my head. I wanted to look around to see Stu nodding at me, putting his thumb up to indicate that he would fly the point, but there was no use in averting my gaze. His thumb was not there to make the decision for me.

"No, Henry." I pitched calmly to Henry, loud enough for him to hear, but gentle enough not to agitate a clamped grouse. If Henry was in two minds, my discouraging tone might be enough stimulus for him to take a couple more steps and assert his point. He remained flat on his belly, poised to pounce.

"Henry, no." My words were wilfully ignored by Henry as he remained motionless, transfixed and unable to give me a stronger indication that grouse were ahead of him. There was only a slight breeze at our altitude, but the clouds were moving high in the sky. Unless Mustard forged hard to break out of the dead air, he'd have little chance of being within touching distance of the grouse. I wasn't too optimistic. *Well, I've done everything you taught me to do, Stu. I can't do much more than take the flight. If not now, then when?* I thought.

I untied Mustard, struck the braces and rolled the hood off. Mustard swelled his feathers as his huge eyes fixed on the horizon and his head remained motionless. Breaking his stare, he bobbed his head as he clocked Henry. His fluffed-up state morphed into a rouse of such vigour that he nearly slipped from the glove. Mustard averted his gaze from the dog, cocked his head skyward, then forward, then skyward again before bursting off the fist, flying right over the top of Henry before pulling up and ascending on his tail. Mustard was very tight in ringing upwards. His presence would certainly have been known to the grouse, who remained clamped as Mustard flew with great purpose. Working hard to get to about 400 feet, he then found a sweet spot of natural uplift and clipped easily, elevating himself to a flickering dot.

That's easily a grand and some. I thought. *This one's for you Stu. Hope you're watching.*

I clicked Henry forward and a pair of grouse clattered out of the heather. Mustard held a perfect tombstone; the spectacle of the stoop was electric, and fried the mournful thoughts I was having. I was captivated watching Mustard fall at fierce velocity and perform a devastating rake through the grouse. He threw up from the crump, quickly inverted, and bound to the poleaxed grouse laying in the heather. By the time I walked over to him, he was busy within a plucked circle of white-tipped, earthy-red feathers. Henry lay next to him as he fed. I took a couple of photos and sent them to Helen and Mandy, with the caption *Mustard's got his grouse.*

Having achieved success with Mustard so early in the tour, I was then at a loss. Continuing for the rest of the week was irredeemably coloured with loneliness. Stu was missing and it felt wrong hawking without him. At the end of the tour, it was surprisingly easy for me to sell both tiercels. They were both well produced, fit gamehawks, which made them desirable. It would be simple for me to ensure they would end up in the hands of someone who would offer them more hunting opportunities than me. I sold the pair of tiercels to a friend of Matt Gage, gave the money to Mandy and had a long winter without falcons, wondering if I'd ever fly one again.

*****

Doubtful

'I have of late, but wherefore I know not, lost all my mirth. And indeed, it goes so heavily with my disposition, that this goodly frame, the Earth, seems to me a sterile promontory...'

–Withnail & I.

I found myself thinking about Withnail reciting *Hamlet.* I could easily have gone down such a path of haplessness and booze.

If it wasn't for the generosity of my good friends – this time it was the turn of Louise and Howard – I think I would have let my passion for falconry slide. Louise, with all the stubbornness she could muster from her Yorkshire heritage, refused to let me wallow in self-pity and idle my talents. To reignite the flames, Louise generously gave me the option to pair any combination of her peregrines and would gift the offspring to me. Louise has a keen eye and is wonderfully snobbish when it comes to peregrines. As a result, her aviaries house some of the most striking peregrines, exemplifying (if there could ever be such a thing) a breed standard beyond repute. Howard also recognised that I needed a catalyst to pick myself up, and subsequently loaned me a high-value, hard-to-come-by, very-much sought-after, nine-week-old female black shaheen peregrine.

The shaheen was mine to train and hunt in her juvenile years and return for breeding at three years old. Despite her worth, Howard insisted I should fly her with much liberty and be the only person in the UK (de facto in the world), to be out hunting red grouse with a black shaheen. So I continued practising falconry in the subsequent seasons.

The tiercel's first conquest was a black grouse (non-targeted), and the shaheen was the highest mounting bird I'd ever flown, soaring in gay abandon well beyond the range of the naked eye. Eventually, I focused her attention and caught a grouse with her. I was the only person I know of to have done so with a black shaheen. At that point, I felt I should gush over the flights and my accomplishments, but I found the events fairly unremarkable. Herein lies the issue. From the outside looking in, it was epic. Yet the passion from within had mostly died. Like Withnail, I too had lost all my mirth.

The shaheen developed a love of ascending thermals on fixed wings, and as such, her flights would be long, lengthy, and of substantial altitude. I first discovered this flying her to the drone on a hot breezy day. She surpassed the drone and lure, took herself about 1 km away and continued ascending to 1,800 feet, simply for her own pleasure, getting drunk on thermals. After about 20 minutes, it was obvious I had little control over her as she failed to respond to the animated drone and dangled lure. I thought I would soon be on my toes, chasing her down, so I recovered the drone and loaded it into my truck. She must have been intrigued by the activity and began to drift overhead. Looking up against the blue sky, I just managed to catch the tiniest glimpse of her, blasted my whistle and threw out the wing lure. She fell like a stone in a phenomenally quick stoop.

The next day she was in a similar condition. I put the drone up without a lure on it, hoping that once she levelled with it, she would surpass it and remain up there until I took out the lure below. She did, and some. All I had to go on was the GPS because I had simply lost sight of her. When her marker showed she was directly overhead it was reading 2,436 feet against a bright blue sky. I swung the lure in earnest. She dropped instantly and I managed to catch the last 500 feet or so of her stoop. It was day three of this new flying style and the day prior to going on tour. I invited Lee to watch her fly before we set off in convoy to the bothy. The shaheen went to 2,818 feet in a 40-minute flight, before plummeting to the lure.

It was tantalising to imagine her stooping from such heights after grouse. For her to achieve this I'd have to fly her a little over-conditioned and out of control on a hot day, then wait for her to look in. On the day of my attempt, we were accompanied by the gamekeeper. Sometimes, falconry can be a terrible spectator sport, and in my attempt to join Hollidge's *Three Grand Club*, I subjected the keeper and the guys to watching a black dot ring up on various hill tops with complete disregard to the planned activity, merrily sightseeing out of my control. Despite my attempts to rein her in that week, I couldn't get her quite set overhead, nor busily climbing with menace over the grouse to keep them clamped. I was experiencing exactly what Stu said *"If I can tell the falcon is flying shit, then so will the grouse."* With the Shaheen out of position, the grouse needed no invitation to split. To give the Shaheen credit, what she lacked in commanding position, she made up for in speed. I've never seen a falcon travel across a skyline in a shallow stoop as quickly or as streakily as a black shaheen.

Had I managed to orchestrate the flush when she was rising on thermals overhead it would have been something to behold. Eventually, on a later excursion, she caught her grouse but, alas, whilst the opportunity to fly a Shaheen for two years was an extreme privilege and rarity – something I'll always be indebted to Howard for – I still felt conflicted and cut adrift from the raging obsession I once had. Maybe it was the fact that she didn't belong to me. Maybe I was still raw and mourning the loss of Stu. Regardless, on handing the falcon back to Howard in the winter of 2020, it seemed a good point to leave behind this undertaking, this lost passion, this world I tried to re-enter, for good.

Black shaheen in the Highlands. ©Leopold Armory

*****

It was May 2021, nearly three years since Stu's passing, when I was contacted out of the blue by Clive, Gilbert's owner. I feared it would be news of Gilbert's passing and would send the recent past into the intangible distance. Instead, he had exciting, unexpected news. Gilbert had laid her first fertile egg. Louise wasn't wrong about Clive. He gave me first refusal on Gilbert's chick at a discounted price that I could now afford. Some three weeks later the chick hatched. It was female. Might I be able to reunite our founding line of peregrines with the next generation of pointers in the Highlands? The prospect had me on edge and there was no indecision.

The very thought of training up my first female peregrine falcon, Gilbert's daughter, to hunt grouse over Onwards Henry reignited my lost rage. For the first time since losing Stu, I had a burning desire to rediscover my passion and make my stride that bit longer when I next took to the moor. I needed no reminder of the many eventualities that could make this ambition doubtful – so much so, that when I collected and held the ten-week-old falcon on the glove for the first time, I knew what her name would be...

Doubtful was in fine condition, a markedly bigger beast on the glove than the smaller tiercels I was familiar with. For a start, she weighed about 1 lb heavier, had much thicker toes and longer talons, which consumed my fist. Doubtful had a bulk and strength to her that commanded great reverence. Her feathers were pin-perfect, her talons sharp, and her mannerisms feisty. The leather glove was barely thick enough to protect my hand from her powerful grip and rapturous bite. Her fiery antics made the atmosphere electric and exciting. I was stirred by her nature and was feverish to have her tear up the sky. I could hear Stu's voice. *We want to hunt with the wolf.* She was everything I could have hoped for.

I spent a considerable amount of time taming Doubtful, getting her used to the home environment and the pointers she was yet to learn the purpose of. I knew I would have to curb my enthusiasm to see her fly until this part of the process was completed to a high standard. Over a week or so, Doubtful calmed down considerably and became quite sweet. She was plucky in her investigations of the inanimate objects close to hand: a book, a mobile phone, the endless cups of tea and wet pointer noses that invaded her personal space while manning. Not until I produced a pair of grouse wings from my hawking vest and threw them on the grass did the feisty dragon return. As soon as she glimpsed the brown mottled wings, she set about them, grasping, tearing, gripping and footing them. She was spirited, to say the least!

Aggression to the lure made the continuation training a doddle. Doubtful's recall to the hung lure quickly progressed to a suspended lure from the drone. Within a matter of days, she was flying free, navigating turbulent air and climbing to the drone. I knew she still had more growing to do, but her avid determination to pull the lure out of the sky gave me the opportunity to put plenty of food through her and pile on the muscle. I continued to keep Doubtful focused on fitness and flying style until we took to the moor. I knew as soon as she was in the sky and flying overhead, she would require no invitation for a stoop once there was a fluttering of grouse bursting out of the heather beneath her. By using Henry, I could be extremely confident that I would be honest and produce game for her at the exact moment she pulled overhead.

Heading for the Goldilocks zone. Me, Henry and Doubtful. ©Leopold Armory

It was the first day of the tour. It was a bright September day of blue sky and high pressure, with a 5–8 mph easterly wind; it couldn't be more perfect. We were forced by the wind direction to work in a region we didn't often go to. The area was a gentle slope of heather that led to a steep, wooded ravine dropping off some 300 metres or so further on. It was a reasonable distance to accommodate a stoop, with a fairly low risk of the grouse making it to the edge of the wood. Onwards Henry quartered hard and locked onto point. It was time for Doubtful's debut.

I thought Doubtful might take a while to leave the fist. Without a visual target in the sky, there wasn't a stimulus to make her race off the glove. Doubtful, however, was very fit and had a strong appetite. She was antsy to rev up and eager to get out in the vast landscape. She took off into the wind and began to climb as if she were looking for the drone to appear. Obviously, there was no drone, but Doubtful went up on her tail as if she was closing in on it. She whizzed past 500 feet, then 600 feet, then 700 feet – now it was getting exciting. At about 900 feet she was well over the ravine and had a little look back at me. I fluttered the grouse wings momentarily from my hawking vest and quickly hid them. In getting her attention, she began to tab back to our location and look inward. Now over the start of the wood, I knew she was nicely advanced to bisect the grouse before reaching the treeline. If Doubtful continued flying towards me she would fly past the dog and potentially miss the flush behind her. I wanted her to see everything and learn the game. The lesson was set, and it would be a good one. Making some excitable noises and flailing my arms around to keep her focused on me, I went towards Henry and called the flush. A single adult cock bird, in the prime of his life, burst like a bullet and headed towards the wood – right underneath Doubtful. I don't think my grandfather's trench whistle had ever been blown as loudly in its life. To the tune of the blast, Doubtful clipped fast and headed towards us as the grouse went underneath her. Just as I thought she wasn't going to dare; she folded and held a stoop.

This was her first proper stoop at live quarry, which happened to be a formidably fit and fast adult grouse. I feared she was too slow in committing to this grouse. It looked like her aim would miss the point at which she needed to bisect and rake through it. Unlike the lure that dangles from the drone, this target shifts. About halfway down in the stoop her trajectory needed to change as the grouse was going to pass her by. She put in the most stunning twist, which brought her round from a head-on position and corkscrewed her into a tail chase. All this happened in a split second. She wasn't far from the grouse and was gaining as they neared the tree line. The grouse didn't dump as I thought it might. Instead, it went through the tree line and hugged the slope descending down into the valley – this old-timer clearly knew how to shake off wild peregrines, who are very unlikely to risk rattling through a wood and injuring themselves. But Doubtful wasn't wild; she was tenacious and immature, and pursued the grouse into the trees, where we all lost sight of her.

This could play out one of three ways: either she'd crash, she'd pull up, or she'd catch the grouse. I stood for a minute and produced the lure, waiting. Next, I fumbled for my phone and tracked the flight from when Doubtful entered the wood. The GPS showed a straight line running through the tree line, but the signal was stationary to the side of a tree a little way up the bank on the opposite side of the ravine, about two kilometres away. I spied the tree as best I could, but I was shaking with adrenaline, and sweat was smearing on the glass of the binoculars. There was no discernible peregrine-shaped outline on the tree, nor was there any movement. I was a little torn. If she had managed to kill her first grouse, I needed to get there pretty quickly to guard her. But if she was in the tree, I'd much rather recall her than recover her myself. It was a considerable descent through pine wood, and there was a tricky scree-faced embankment to negotiate. There would be no getting back up it once at the bottom. The GPS remained fixed and there was no response to the swinging lure, so there was nothing for it other than to head straight down. I shouted back to the chaps and arranged a rendezvous point. The closest a vehicle could get to the GPS fix was about 500 metres away. I set off in a straight line to the GPS fix. I got within about 250 metres, scanned again with my binoculars and still couldn't see her in the tree. A flickering of a wing got my attention and I managed to spot her near the base of the tree. Doubtful was struggling to stand, wings outstretched, scrabbling in a deep patch of rank heather. Had she done it? It would have been pretty epic for her to stack into the heather to grab a grouse. Had she got it at her feet?

I picked up the pace. Doubtful was in her most exposed and vulnerable state, a very easy target for a buzzard or eagle. Flailing her wings like that was a tempting proposition for any raptor to stack in and kill her, especially if they presumed she had a kill in her feet. As I made it to within about 100m of Doubtful, she scrambled some more, then took off and headed straight towards me. *Arghhh,* no grouse. She must have been so close and aggressively committed into the heather where the grouse had sought cover. Doubtful probably locked her feet on the heather stems and the stimulus and adrenaline held them grasped while I was making my way to her. Regardless of what might have happened, she was now flying straight to me and took the lure with much venom. She was fired up and took a while to calm down. I rewarded her well for that flight – her first *bloody nearly* – which must have been so exhilarating I was sure she'd be keen for another. With Doubtful secured to the fist, well fed and hooded, it took me about 15 minutes to make my way to the track and get a lift back up the hill.

Throughout the week, Doubtful was incredible to watch. Every flight with her was impressive and she came excruciatingly close to catching a grouse. Although she didn't manage it, the flying style and stoops were electric. Doubtful's benchmark stoop came from about a grand each time, and the lowest I served her from during the whole tour was about 850 feet. From these pitches, she'd pursue grouse with such perseverance it was thrilling to watch her and the incredible evasive measures taken by her quarry in this challenging, undulating environment.

Onwards Henry and Doubtful ✎Amelia Siddle

On the final weekend of the tour, Mandy and Sam drove up and joined us. Stu had been too long in the urn on Mandy's sideboard. It was high time we spread his ashes on the moor, as he'd requested. For the occasion I had bought a beautiful native mountain ash (also known as a rowan tree) and snuck it into an area of natural regeneration woodland at the hill foots, just visible from the track on the way up to Peregrine Rock. There were no other rowans nearby, so I was a little worried someone might spot its tree protector and the small cairn of rocks placed round its delicate trunk and remove it. Mountain ash is steeped in mythology and it's very bad luck to tamper with a rowan. I hoped folklore might prevent its disappearance.

When a rowan is found out of place, somewhere where it seemingly has no licence to be, typically in a crag or beside a stream far from any other, its seed likely deposited by bird droppings, it is called a 'flying rowan', which I felt most appropriate. Stu would evermore be under his 'flying rowan', and greeted each time we passed on our way up the hill. Not only do grouse and many other birds feed from the berries of the rowan – we would also be able to use the ripe September berries to flavour alcohol and make jelly to complement our game dishes. There was no better or more fitting memorial.

Spreading Stu's ashes was a very relaxing, therapeutic affair. We laughed as much as we cried, and sat around while a few of our favourite stories and memories were bandied about. It was the only time we had all been to the moor and not hawked. We were carefree, unexpectant, and basking in the stunning scenery – it was magic. As we polished off a bottle of sloe gin between us, the midges began to appear, which marked the end of ceremonies and the tour. We bumbled down off the hill, had a final night in the bothy and said our goodbyes before heading home.

One week after the tour I would be turning 40. There was nothing I'd rather have done to mark this milestone than to get a flight with Doubtful. My old mate Mike joined me; we headed to the moor and had another *bloody nearly*. A grouse in the bag would have been a great birthday treat but, alas, that gift would be reserved for another day. Driving back in the truck, catching up properly with Mike, he told me his son was turning seven next year –

the same age that Mike was introduced to falconry. I wondered whether the following season was the time to get him out for a stoop on grouse – or did we know better? Should we perhaps protect him from this addictive, rollercoaster lifestyle? Snooker or golf instead, perhaps? Mike told me he still had the same Nimrod falconry glove he was given all those Christmases ago. "I think it's time to see if the glove fits the next generation," he said.

"Speaking of the next generation, there's a quick stop I need to make on the way home," I told Mike with a smile on my face. We swung into the service station where I had arranged to collect a beautiful and lovingly reared pup at eight weeks old. She was Onwards Henry's daughter. As things were coming full circle, I decided to name her Jess, after Stu's dog. There are some birthday presents that money can't buy.

Onwards

As I write this in the autumn 2023 it has been five years since Stu's passing and some fifteen years since I first met him. Although I only knew him for a relatively short time – 10 years – I am, like all those who knew Stu, left to reflect. To me, Stu was a zeitgeist of falconry as well as someone who displayed joy and kindness in the purest form I've ever known. He remained vehemently true to himself, his values, his ethics, and bravely authentic in the face of heartache and adversity until his last breath. Stu would always do as much as he could to support those closest to him, and was never shy to offer up advice; rarely was he wrong. Aside from the falconry mentoring he gave, his biggest influence was affirming that chasing money and riches is a horrible aspiration. When we fade into old age, if our greatest achievement to reflect on is a figure on a calculator screen, then that is a sorrowful, unfulfilling and regrettable way to end.

Stu once told me a story of a man who came to his door and tried to buy Cody. The man wouldn't stop bidding and became increasingly frustrated when his offers failed to secure him the dog. Everything has a price, right? Not for a man who disdained money and loved his dogs. When the offers got stupid and went north of £8k, Stu told the man in no uncertain terms that, unless he stopped bidding up, he would knock him out and put him in his wheelie bin. Stu smiled at me in recounting the story, his eyes wore an authoritative knowing look that shone with contentment and righteousness. Stu had something that that man would never, ever have: enough. Stu had enough, and was satisfied with enough.

I was understandably floored when Stu passed. I still feel a huge sense of injustice at him not being here. The emotion makes me well up when I reflect on the time we spent together. I still really do miss him. Immediately after he passed, I struggled to pick myself up and get going again; there seemed little point in hawking without him. The four influences that nudged me further on the healing process, and gave me some sense of reconciliation, were:

(i) The unrelenting stare of Onwards Henry. This pointer of physical perfection and determined mindset would rest his chin on my thigh. Looking back at him, there was no fibre within me that could deny him his desire to forge across the moor and connect with grouse. I took the lead made from Henry Worsley's sled ropes, threw them over my dog and was dragged to the moor to count grouse. Each time we set foot on heather, my legs began to free themselves. Once again I'd look in fascination at this environment and reconnect my fieldcraft to the landscape.

(ii) I heard an old fable that described a couple running to escape a flood. Fleeing the torrent, they crossed the street, but in doing so became trapped when their ankles caught in a storm drain. The rain poured down and the water level rose, drowning the husband. The difference between the deceased and the widow? The man was too stubborn to bow down and cut off that part of him that would hold him under. I knew unless I took measures to rid myself of grief and get on with life, I too would be consumed.

(iii) A quote by Richard Dawkins, evolutionary biologist and author, which reads *'We are going to die, and that makes us the lucky ones. Most people are never going to die because they are never going to be born... In the teeth of these stupefying odds it is you and I, in our ordinariness, that are here. We privileged few, who won the lottery of birth against all odds, how dare we whine at our inevitable return to that prior state from which the vast majority have never stirred?'* [4] Dawkins' words make for rather frank, unsympathetic reading for the recently bereaved. Yet once I'd reflected on these words, they served up honest tough love and the realisation that my sorrowful self-pitying state needed to be repurposed to appreciative thankfulness, however hard that might be.

(iv) I was blindly stuck in traffic on the Edinburgh bypass on the 7th September 2020, two years after Stu had died. It was towards the beginning of the hawking season. I was en route to the moor with eager pointers and peregrines, very much still discontented about practising falconry without Stu. Enjoying myself when flying a hawk after his passing somehow seemed disrespectful and vulgar. I put on the radio and found myself listening to an

4.   Unweaving the Rainbow: Science, Delusion and the Appetite for Wonder. Richard Dawkins

interview with Vinnie Jones. He was discussing the loss of Tanya, his wife of 25 years. His was the voice of a broken, but slowly healing man. A far cry from the alpha-dog visionary I had in my mind's eye. 'Big Chris' of *Lock, Stock and Two Smoking Barrels* or 'Bullet-Tooth Tony' of *Snatch*. I could hear both characters, but I was listening to Vinnie. He talked with such conviction and sincerity.

Vinnie realised he was masking too much when talking to Geoff Shreeves; Geoff noted "You're smiling through your mouth, not your eyes." Vinnie then went on to describe the guilt he associated with being happy, that it seemed wrong to laugh after such devastation. This was exactly how I felt, and the sentiment was strongest when I was practising falconry. Vinnie continued, impressing the importance of finding joyous grief, allowing yourself to laugh in a mournful state, then eventually, hopefully, being able to do so uncontrollably once more.

Continuing the pilgrimage without Stu seemed drab. While I was outwardly smiling, internally I was largely unenthused, resentful of being there without him. I missed him dearly. Thankfully, the camaraderie, support, unrelenting and outrageous humour of the chaps kept chipping away at me to the point where I now long for the tour and the company of Ken McDougall, John Hatchett, Lee McGrorty and Dave Bishop. These stalwarts have been essential to my recovery. Together, we've naturally developed a selfless friendship and team mentality which sees each of our prodigal peregrines and pointers progress through the ranks as we marvel at them in full tilt across the mountain range. The standard of gamehawking we produce is incredible and we exact Stu's vision of a close syndicate. With Stu's ashes buried under his 'flying rowan', along with his pointers, the moor has a great magnetic spirit, where familiar ghosts walk with us, quarter ahead of us, observe and influence every spectacle – it is a calling we now long for. The season after I learned about joyous grief from Vinnie, I was striding with purpose, across the moor, with Doubtful on my fist.

*****

Stu's influence still guides me in the field. I laugh when I remember things that amused him – like the delight he took in deliberately driving in the middle of a convoy so he didn't have to get out to open or close a gate. Each year I'm reduced to a heavy-hearted state when I drive the track to Peregrine Rock and pass Stu's flying rowan. However, knowing he is resting at peace in his utopia brings huge comfort. He guards the canvas on which we embrace his memory and enjoy the freedom to revel in our heritage. Had I given up and rejected the support of those closest to me, I would never have gained closure. The acute intricacies of life would never have been allowed to come full circle, and be dearly cherished. It required resilience, progression and Herculean strength to re-forge the broken ends. So then, Onwards.

Stu, now *waiting on* in peace. 📷©Leopold Armory

*****

Dedicated to Stuart Fall… See, I promised to tell them what you were like.

Acknowledgements

"Passion for something can easily tip into obsession, which is a dangerous thing, especially when those affected are the very people who so loyally stand and wait."

–Henry Worsley

As soon as I read Henry's quote, one name (the most important name) screamed through the text – **Kerry Warren** – my wife. She has been at the coalface, suffered and endured everything associated with being a falconer's wife. In spite of this, she still continues to accept, support and (sometimes) encourage me to pursue this rage. Falconry can be a selfish, potent addiction. Being late to her birthday party when I thought it sensible and necessary to fly the shaheen off the creance for the first time is just one such example. Still, the 4 hours standing under the tree in which it alighted gave me time to reflect. *Shaheens can be such good liars…* I thought.

In some folklore, mothers of unruly, disobedient daughters will curse their child by wishing their future husband be a falconer – I can see why! On top of tolerating my pointers, peregrines, collateral, obsessive mind-set and impulsive, imperative trips to the field, Kerry also supported me throughout my grief and my frustrations in getting this book over the line. She looks after me better than I do myself. On the promise that she would never try to curtail my rage, Stu gave Kerry his approval to our being wed. I would have given anything to have him at our wedding.

The most profound yet inadvertent compliment I have *ever* received is the recounted words of Professor T. M. A. Wilson, a stranger to me at the time. In the hope that Wilson would be kind enough to provide some much-needed editorial assistance, I gave him a draft copy of *Onwards*, on which to scrawl with his famed red pen. It later got back to me that, having read the draft, he said "Dave Warren, you'd want him in your lifeboat." I loved hearing that, and sincerely hope he is at the wrong end of a bottle of Châteauneuf-du-Pape reading this.

I am blessed to have a small, solid group of messrs who have encouraged, supported and made it possible for me to write *Onwards*. We fly in and out of each other's lives, depending on circumstance, each time as if we had spoken just moments earlier.

In *my* lifeboat are:

My Parents, always encouraging me to pursue interests oh so foreign to them, spurring me on to be the rogue sheep of the family and to live a life that pleases me. **Mike Coles,** still my oldest and best friend; we share a rich humour born from our childhood, and he knows me better than any other. Author **Dr. Andrew Dobson,** the voice of rational, logical consideration and a bloody good giggle to boot. Not only a fine housemate in The Box, but the sole influence I had for writing this book. **Phil Savage**, a man who works harder than anyone I know, yet always takes time for me and shows huge kindness in making my endeavours a reality. Longstanding friend **Louise Baggley**, a forthright Yorkshire lass who says it like it is. Despite not suffering fools gladly, she has put up with me and been my sounding-board over many years. **Howard Waller** and **Clive Stancer,** who, without reason to be so kind to me, generously enabled me to do more than I can ever thank them for. They kept the precious flames alive so that the inferno could rage once more. **Dr. Paul Dayus Cooke,** the humble son of a great man. My closest friend since childhood. He is the voice in my head and always a great inspiration. Not only does he make life happen for him, he's a fighter, a scrapper, and along the way, has always shared the spoils with me.

The *Peregrines over Pointers* stalwarts. These fine gentlemen put me back on the horse after losing Stu. I crave their company in the field and now long for the tour. I can't thank them enough for their kindness, support and camaraderie. **Dave Bishop**, good friend to Stu and there throughout. In the face of adversity, Bish just keeps going, always with something funny to say. **John Hatchet,** a true working-class hero. His devilish sense of humour is at odds with his sincere and kind nature. Despite often being up a ladder cleaning windows, he's one of the most grounded men I know. **Ken McDougal,** his cute wit is paired with a keen eye and vision for pointers and peregrines; this makes him not only a proponent, but a cherished and favoured hawking buddy. **Lee McGrorty,** his de-facto mindset is figuring out a way to help others. He never commands success but always selflessly enables it. Tirelessly, he goes above and beyond to help those in front of him achieve. **Leopold Armory,** with us from the outset, dedicated to his craft and his pursuit of a rural photographic portfolio beyond compare. He's forged up hills in order to take the most stunning imagery, and in doing so, captured the most precious keepsake photographs we all treasure. **Andrew Hollidge,** his airborne achievements flying hang gliders are as remarkable as the peregrines he produces. Unfortunately, these commitments clash with the tour dates; nevertheless, without him, the story would never have been told. He was a great friend to Stu. **Manders and Sam Fall,** we share our grief and loss, but also our healing and reflection. Givers of much warmth and kind-hearted affection. I'll never forget laying Stu to rest on the moor with you. Thank you for your encouragement and support with *Onwards.* **Max Worsley,** adventurous but always glancing back. Thoughtful, kind and sentimental – a chip off the old block – and extremely encouraging of my writing, thank you.

My Influences growing up – **Reverend Payne**, it is fun to be back in touch after all this time, remembering village life with great fondness. **Richard Clarke,** forever 'The Boss' in my eyes. An unbelievable influence in developing work ethic, drive, responsibility and ownership, with **Jackie Clarke** and **Kev Nash.**

The guinea pigs to whom I force-fed my sample writing: **Lauren McGough, Amy Woods, Laura Wrede, Krista Hong Edwards** and **Diana Durman Walters** all nurtured my apprehension and fuelled the confidence to continue. Those who lent editorial assistance: **Richard Roper, Craig Adams, Professor T. M. A. Wilson and Rebecca Warren.** Each helped to unfold the story in a colourful, entertaining and poignant way – ensuring that the peregrine, pointer and grouse is the thread, but the human story and lifestyle remains the fabric. As such, with the fondest of memories, we remember:

Henry Worsley, MBE. Stuart Fall. Roy Coles. Professor Matt Gage.

Not least, I'd like to thank **Thomas van Straubenzee** for his endorsement. I'm still amazed by his generosity, encouragement and morale-boosting influence in getting this book over the line.

*****

©Leopold Armory

Contributing Artists:

Andrew Halsen (front cover):

Andrew Halsen was born in Essex in 1953. In 1977, he was given the opportunity to train and fly a peregrine falcon. It was this falcon, Tassa, that Ray Turner wrote about in his classic monograph *Gamehawk*, which was illustrated by Halsen. Halsen's work, in many cases, are not highly finished but are deliberately sketch-like in their execution, giving fleeting glimpses of pheasants, partridges, ducks and grouse as the falcon strikes them. They are studies from the perspective of the hunter and the hunted.

During his career, Andrew has won several awards, including: The Royal Society for Nature Conservation 'Natural World' Art Award, 1992 & 1997, and runner-up in 1993. The Royal Society for the Protection of Birds Art Award, 1996 and 1999. His work has been exhibited at the Leigh Yawkey Woodson Art Museum, Wisconsin U.S.A. Other shows include Birds in Art, 1993 (work purchased by the Museum), Birds in Art, 1995, and The Artist's View, 1996.

Amelia Siddle (rear cover):

Born in 1991 and largely self taught, Siddle's main inspiration is the dog. Siddle considers herself lucky enough to have grown up surrounded by what she considers to be one of the most beautiful breeds – the Pointer – which she describes as 'the thoroughbred and aristocrat of the canine world', and a subject that taught her an in-depth knowledge of canine anatomy, movement and balance.

Siddle's work resides in both public and private collections all over the world, with multiple pieces owned by The Kennel Club and on display in Clarges Street, London, most notably a hallmarked silver sculpture commissioned by the Crufts dog show committee in 2016. Siddle finds a deep enjoyment in capturing the fluidity of movement and energy in each piece, showing the essence and individuality of each subject, in a variety of mediums.

April Coppini:

Born and raised in a wooded suburb of Rochester, New York, April attended the University of the Arts in Philadelphia in 1990, and Alfred University, School of the Arts, from 1991-1994. She received her BFA from Alfred in printmaking and drawing, and moved to Portland, Oregon in 1995. April works at her home studio in North-East Portland, where she lives with her family and finds inspiration from her three children, cat Frank, two rescued dogs – Stevie and Rogue – and a big, wild garden visited by several different species of flying, hopping and crawling things.

[A personal note from me] April not only produces exceptional sketches of wolves, but in my eyes, personifies the phrase 'wolf mother'. I implore all readers of this to check out her inspirational story; maybe you can help? The power, strength and resolve that April conveys on paper is just a deft depiction of her mindset.

Contributing Photographers:

Leopold Armory:

Bio-less. (remarkably).

Although his work speaks for itself, it's my suspicion that Leo's probably too reserved to write a bio, choosing instead to immerse in the Highlands and spend his time being a good friend to so many. Leo doesn't cheat in the authenticity of his photographs; he will wild camp in blizzards, lie in the shallows of the River Dee to await crossing stags, and risk exhaustion and exposure so that his work remains honest and beautiful.

I first met Leo at a time when he was sleeping in the back of his van, next to his camera. He had made the decision to travel to the Highlands, penniless, to capture its beauty. He had a stale baguette and some cheese, and was nervous to ask if it was an imposition for him to boil some eggs in our bothy. We all took an instant liking to this man and his nature, Stu especially. Thus, reading a self-written vanity piece is inappropriate. Instead, it is fitting you discover his talents by visiting his Instagram.

Sebastian Copeland:

Sebastian Copeland is a polar explorer, climate advocate, photographer and author. In 2017, Sebastian was named one of the world's 25 Most Adventurous Men of the last 25 years by Men's Journal.

Sebastian won the prestigious International Photography Awards (IPA) Photographer of the Year twice for his books: first *Antarctica: A Global Warning* (Palace Press) in 2007, and again in 2020 for *Antarctica: The Waking Giant* (Rizzoli). He also won the Tokyo International Foto Awards (TIFA) Photographer of the Year twice: in 2015 for *Arctica: The Vanishing North* (teNeues), which also won the ITB Book Award and the Global Arctic Award, and in 2021, for *Antarctica: The Waking Giant* (Rizzoli).

Neil Aldridge:

Neil is a conservationist, photographer and filmmaker, as well as a professional wildlife guide, speaker and author. His photography has won awards all over the world, including winning the World Press environment category, the overall title of European Wildlife Photographer of the Year and the NPPA's Best of Photojournalism award for environmental storytelling.

Printed in Great Britain
by Amazon

39765003R00109